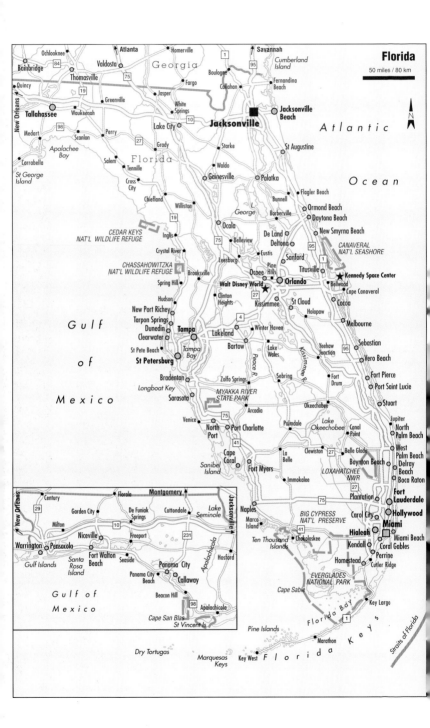

FLORIDA

APA PUBLICATIONS
Part of the Langenscheidt Publishing Group

introduction

Welcome

This guidebook combines the interests and enthusiasms of two of the world's best-known information providers: Insight Guides, who have set the standard for visual travel guides since 1970, and Discovery Channel, the world's premier source of non-fiction television programming.

Its aim is to help visitors make the most of their stay in the land of magic kingdoms, offbeat islands, honky-tonk beach towns, Cuban exiles, sun-tanned surfers, Native Americans, ocean breezes, plastic flamingoes and orange perfume.

To this end, Insight's correspondent in Florida, Joann Biondi, has devised a series of 17 tailor-made tours based on four key areas: Orlando in the center of the state, with its world-renowned theme parks; the Tampa/St Petersburg area in the west, with its lovely beaches; exotic Miami in the south with its art deco architecture and Cuban associations; and from there the Florida Keys, with their funky, laid-back atmosphere. Supporting the itineraries are sections on history and culture, shopping, eating out, nightlife and a calendar of special events, plus a fact-packed practical information section, with a list of hand-picked hotels.

Joann Biondi has lived and worked as a journalist in Florida since the 1970s. She says there is no place in the world she would rather live. 'I like hearing the wild parrots that squawk each morning, going for a swim on New Year's Eve, and picking fresh oranges from the tree in my yard. I've had northerners ask, "How can you live there," and others say, "I wish I were you." It is a place that makes you realize that making a life is more important than making a living.' With the help of the itineraries and recommendations in this guide, Joann hopes that some of her love of Florida will rub off on you.

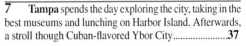

Pages 2/3: Miami's famous beach
Pages 8/9: the Scorpion ride at Busch Gardens

History & *Culture*

The modern-day tourists, positioning their beach towels so that they get their fair share of Florida sunshine, are just the latest in a long line of pilgrims who believe that they too are entitled to a small slice of the state. For centuries, Florida has attracted conquerors, settlers, developers, dreamers, escapees, refugees, immigrants, and travelers. It is a place where people come for rest, rejuvenation, retirement. And to start anew.

In the beginning there were Native Americans. Timucuans, Calusas, Apalachees, Tequestas, Mayaimas, Apalachicolas, Miccosukees, and Seminoles. But, as in most parts of the Americas, the tribes were no match for the European settlers who came to conquer the land and the peoples they found on it. Juan Ponce de León, sailing under the Spanish flag, was the first explorer credited with 'discovering' Florida, in 1513. Continuing the Spanish conquest, de León was followed by Panfilo de Narvaez and Hernando de Soto who both sailed into Tampa Bay. Then came another Spaniard, Pedro Menendez de Aviles, who in 1565 founded St Augustine, the oldest city in the US. For a brief period in the mid-16th century there was a small French settlement near St Augustine, but it was quickly destroyed by the Spaniards, who detested the 'French pirates.' In the 300 years that followed, the Spanish and the British vied for control of the Florida peninsula.

By the 19th century, Florida was a haven for runaway slaves fleeing the South. Only in 1821 did the United States gain control of the peninsula. Thereafter Americans began staking their claims to land along the banks of the Miami River.

The Dade Massacre

The mid-19th century was marked by a series of Seminole Indian Wars, as the tribes tried to resist what the white settlers called progress. About 1,500 slaves joined the Seminole tribe and fought alongside the Native Americans against the settlers. One of the most notable confrontations was the Dade Massacre in which Major Francis L Dade (after whom Miami's county was named) was killed. When Florida became a state in 1845, the population totaled 87,000, including 39,000 black slaves.

When the American Civil War broke out in 1861, Florida mustered its minuscule population and its even smaller budget to join the conflict alongside the Confederate South. Its participation was brief and limited, but devastating. By the time the South surrendered in 1865, much of developed Florida had been destroyed by the Union troops. It did not take long to recover due to the arrival, in the 1860s and '70s, of the first northern developers,

Left: steaming up the Oklawaha River in the 19th century
Right: Hernando de Soto sailed into Tampa Bay

whose names are now immortalized in numerous local street signs. The northeners were here to claim their stake, especially in Miami.

In the second half of the 19th century, Florida experienced a substantial increase in population and a subsequent growth in building and development. In 1880, the state's population had soared to around 270,000, and the

land boom that would stretch into the 1920s had begun. Five years later the American Medical Association endorsed the St Petersburg area as the healthiest region in the entire country.

Railroad Tycoons

Two railroad tycoons were responsible for a significant proportion of Florida's early growth. Henry M Flagler, a retired northern oil baron, decided that Florida was not only up for grabs, but was his for the taking. Flagler built a series of palatial hotels and created the Florida East Coast Railroad to deliver tourists to their doors. He started his first Florida hotel in St Augustine in 1885, and by 1896 had extended his resort building and railroad tracks to Miami. In 1912 his train roared into Key West. At about the same time Henry B Plant was busy developing Florida's west coast. Plant built the Atlantic Coastline Railroad that linked Richmond, Virginia, with Tampa, and then constructed the luxurious Tampa Bay Hotel to attract wealthy tourists.

The early years of the 20th century brought more growth. The architect Addison Mizner built a playground for the richest of the rich in Palm Beach; millionaire Carl Fisher turned what was nothing more than a barren sandbar into the resort paradise known as Miami Beach; property developer George Merrick created the beautiful Mediterranean-style city of Coral Gables near Miami. Life in Florida, especially in the south, was looking great until two hurricanes, in 1926 and 1928, wreaked havoc on the southern part of the state. The stock market crash of 1929, followed by the Great Depression, added more misery to Florida's beleaguered citizenry.

By the outbreak of World War II in 1939, the state's population had reached

2 million, and some 2½ million tourists were visiting Florida every year. After the war, more and more tourists began to head south for a much-needed vacation. Throughout the 1940s, '50s and '60s, hundreds of small motels and quirky roadside attractions sprung up across the state. Families from all over America made the long drive down the highways to Florida. They visited alligator zoos, pineapple farms, and broad, empty beaches. In its early years, Florida's tourism industry, although already seen as the golden egg of future prosperity, was simple, wholesome, and authentic.

Meanwhile the state was benefiting from the development of a thoroughly 20th-century industry: the exploration of space. Florida was the ideal location for this exciting new field on account not only of its climate but due to its position next to the ocean, which could serve as a buffer zone should something go awry. Cape Canaveral began launching missiles into space in the late 1940s. In an attempt to keep up with the Soviet Union's space explorations, the US government poured billions of dollars into its Florida-based space program, and it launched its first satellite, *Explorer I*, in 1958. It was from Cape Canaveral (now called the Kennedy Space Center) that astronaut Neil Armstrong blasted off for the moon in 1969. The space program, a tourist attraction in itself, provides many jobs and is undoubtedly an important economic asset for the state.

Other prominent contributors to the state's economy are agriculture, cattle, and international banking. And about two-thirds of the nation's citrus fruits – oranges, grapefruits, lemons, limes, and tangerines – come from Florida. The vast orange groves of central Florida alone produce about 250 million crates of oranges and 800 million gallons of orange juice a year. So it's easy to understand why a cold spell in winter (which doesn't happen too often) worries not only the tourist trade but farmers too.

Enter Mickey Mouse

One of the most dramatic changes in modern Florida's history occurred in 1971, the year that Mickey Mouse came to town. The opening of Walt Disney World south of Orlando forever altered the atmosphere of Florida and transformed its tourism industry from a small-scale, mom-and-pop business into a multinational, mass-market giant like no other in the world. Along with Mickey Mouse came more and more enormous hotels, fast-food restaurants, super-highways, expanded airports, and junky souvenir shops selling glittery mouse ears. Following in Disney's path came a new genre of tourist attraction in Florida: self-contained, expensive theme parks of fantasyland fun.

Since then Florida has become the fourth most populous state in the US,

Above Left: Railroad tycoon Henry M Flagler. **Left:** On track for economic growth
Above: Palm Beach as seen on a 1954 postcard

with today's total reaching almost 15 million. The internal migration of American retirees, which started over 50 years ago, is never-ending. After spending a lifetime working hard in the northeast or Midwest, many senior citizens feel that retirement in Florida is their due reward as they reach the last leg of the American dream. Much of the state's elderly population live in retirement communities, and condominiums, designed specifically to meet their needs, have sprouted up across the state. 'Snowbirds' (people who come for the winter) are another Florida phenomenon. Once predominantly American, the snowbirds of recent years include wealthy visitors from around the world and sun-seeking celebrities who own extravagantly apportioned vacation home here.

Spanish Supersedes English

Following the Cuban revolution of 1959, refugees fleeing the Communist takeover of their island began streaming into the state. In recent decades more than a million Cubans have left their homeland – many of them via small, rubber rafts – and settled down to start new lives in Florida. Their

presence, especially in south Florida, has pumped young blood into the economy, and radically changed the state's ethnic make-up. Furthermore, hundreds of thousands of Nicaraguans, Guatemalans, Venezuelans, and Colombians have migrated to Florida, swelling the Latin American population to such a degree that in some areas Spanish is spoken more than English. Florida has also received a large number of West Indian immigrants in the past 20 years, including Jamaicans, Haitians, and Bahamians

Top: It's off to work we go for Mickey Mouse and seven construction laborers
Above: a family of Haitian immigrants joins many other newcomers to the state

who have added yet more multicultural spice to the state's rich ethnic mix.

Old-fashioned Florida Crackers – as the descendants of early white settlers are commonly known – are an endangered species, but can still be found, especially in the central and northern parts of the state. What's left of the Seminole and Miccosukee populations in Florida tend to live on self-contained reservations that are scattered across the state. Many of these reservations have, somewhat controversially, been transformed into money-making tourist attractions that sell arts and crafts. Some of the reservations, where the laws that regulate gambling in the rest of the state do not apply, now offer bingo games as another way to generate income.

The city of Orlando has enjoyed unprecedented growth, due in large part to Walt Disney World and its theme-park neighbors. The new arrivals are not merely tourists; in the past 10 years the population of the three counties that straddle Orlando has swelled by 102 people *per day*. Major industries have followed suit, with the American Automobile Association, AT&T, and Westinghouse setting up shop within a few years of each other. In this time the Orlando area has created more factory jobs than any other place in the United States, and employment has risen by almost 150 percent.

An unwelcome visitor by the name of Andrew arrived on Florida's shores in August 1992. In four terrifying hours, this category-five hurricane, packing 160-mph (260-kph) winds and a 12-ft (3.7-meter) tidal surge, slammed into south Florida, destroying more than 60,000 homes and leaving 150,000 people homeless. The worst natural disaster ever to hit the US, Andrew left a 25-mile (40-km) wide path of destruction to the tune of $30 billion. Hardest hit were the rural areas of Homestead, Florida City, and Kendall, about 20 miles (32km) south of downtown Miami. Fortunately for the area's tourism industry, most of Miami's main attractions suffered only minimal damage. Although the rebuilding of the devastated areas is expected to take decades – and was not helped by more severe weather and flooding in March 1993 – residents throughout the state pitched in to help their neighbors to the south.

A Boy Named Elian

In November 1999 (symbolically enough on Thanksgiving Day), two fishermen found a five-year-old Cuban boy clinging to an inner tube just off the coast of south Florida. After a daring escape from Cuba and the sinking of his 17-ft (5-meter) boat, little Elian Gonzalez could only watch as his mother and several other passengers drowned at sea. In a tale that took on epic proportions, Elian claimed that friendly dolphins surrounded him at sea and protected him from marauding sharks. Although he was welcomed with open arms by his Miami relatives and cheered by the Miami Cuban community, Elian quickly became the focus of a bitter custody battle that mesmerized the nation and engulfed

Right: the category-five Hurricane Andrew devastated parts of Florida in 1992

two long-hostile nations – the US and Cuba – in tense legal and political maneuverings. He also set in motion a series of ethnic clashes between Miami's Cubans and its other citizens. At one point a group of non-Cuban protestors derisively tossed bunches of bananas at Miami City Hall.

Meanwhile Elian was showered with gifts from his Miami relatives, and was taken to Disney World, where he shook hands with Mickey Mouse. Throughout the controversy, the little boy at its center was paraded in front of the media circus camped outside his relatives' Little Havana house. Seven months after his arrival, federal agents stormed the Little Havana home in

an early-morning raid and forcefully removed Elian from his relatives' custody. After a brief stop in Washington, DC, where his father, Juan Miguel Gonzalez, was waiting for him, Elian flew home to Cuba and eventually returned to the simple life he had known in the small town of Cárdenas.

Election Fever

Media-savvy Florida ordinarily welcomes any free publicity that comes its way, but the US presidential election of 2000, the closest such contest in 124 years, brought a slew of unwanted notoriety to the Sunshine State. The legal and electoral turmoil over the slender margin that separated the Democrat contender Al Gore and his Republican rival George W Bush in Florida dragged on for 36 days. Amid the mayhem were charges of partisan politics, a rigged system, poorly designed ballots, sloppy vote counting, mishandled absentee ballots, dilapidated punch card machines, and racial discrimination at the voting booths. The result of the Florida election – and the all-important 25 electoral votes it represented – had the power to determined the outcome of the entire election, and as a result the eyes of the world were focused on the little north Florida capital city of Tallahassee. The political discourse and media scrutiny was so painful, that the entire state grew thoroughly weary.

Eventually the US Supreme Court ruled against a recount of the Florida ballots and George W ('Dubya') Bush officially won Florida and thus the presidency. What the tortuous fiasco revealed was that this state, known to many only for its pastel facades and fantasy vacations, indeed had serious problems in its electoral system. However, as has been seen in other times of state-wide crisis, Floridians never lost their sense of humor, and even came up with a new batch of bumper stickers. Among the best were:

Florida: If you think we can't vote, wait till you see us drive
Florida: Home of electile dysfunction
Florida: This is what you get for taking Elian Gonzalez away from us
Florida: We've been Gored by the bull of politics and now we're Bushed
Florida: Relax, Retire, Revote!

Above: the Cuba Memorial in Miami's Little Havana

HISTORY HIGHLIGHTS

5000BC An unknown, aboriginal culture inhabits the northern part of the Florida peninsula, subsisting on fishing, hunting, and agriculture.

AD300–1000 Highly developed Native American tribes inhabit many parts of the peninsula.

1498 Cartographer John Cabot, sailing on behalf of the British, draws a crude map of Florida.

1513 Spanish explorer Juan Ponce de León discovers Florida while searching for the island of Bimini.

1521 De León returns with 200 settlers.

1565 St Augustine, the oldest city in the US, is founded by Pedro Menendez de Aviles of Spain.

1763–83 The British accept Florida from Spain in exchange for Havana; following the Revolutionary War, Britain trades Florida back to Spain.

1821 The US gains control of Florida from Spain and hundreds of runaway slaves from the north settle in Florida.

Mid-19th Century A series of Seminole Wars erupts as Native American tribes try to hold on to their land.

1845 Florida becomes a US state.

1861 As an important slave-holding state, Florida secedes from the Union and joins the southern Confederacy in preparation for the American Civil War.

1865 The Civil War ends, costing Florida $20 million in damages and more than 5,000 lives.

1885 Immigration from Cuba increases as a wave of Cuban cigar makers settles in Tampa.

1896 Henry M Flagler's Florida East Coast Railroad from St Augustine to Miami opens. In 1912 it continues on to Key West.

1915 Miami Beach becomes a city. Casinos and cafés flourish.

1920s A so-called land-boom envelops the state; houses and hotels are built throughout Florida.

1928 A hurricane kills more than 2,000 people near Lake Okeechobee.

1930s Art Deco hotels go up in Miami Beach and tourism begins to thrive in south Florida.

1947 Cape Canaveral launches its first series of missiles into space.

1950s Internal migration and large-scale tourism begins.

1959 Fidel Castro takes control of Cuba and triggers a massive influx of Cuban refugees to Florida.

1964 Civil Rights Act. Blacks in Florida begin to overcome severe racial discrimination and segregation.

1970s US economic recession hits Florida. President Nixon vacations on Key Biscayne as four Miamians instigate the Watergate scandal. Conditions in the Caribbean island of Haiti worsen and thousands of Haitians sail on rickety boats to Miami.

1971 Walt Disney World opens near Orlando.

1984 The cool and trendy TV series *Miami Vice* transforms Florida's image.

1992–3 Hurricane Andrew blasts south Florida, leaving 150,000 people homeless; another storm spawns 50 tornados which kill 51 people across the state.

1995 Governor Lawton Chiles files a $1.2 billion lawsuit against the Tobacco Institute for the state's costs in treating Medicare smokers.

1999 Cuban castaway Elian Gonzalaz comes ashore in Florida and foments a bitter international custody fight that lasts seven months.

2000 The US presidential election turns into a messy judicial contest while the eyes of the whole world turn to a vote-counting battle in Florida.

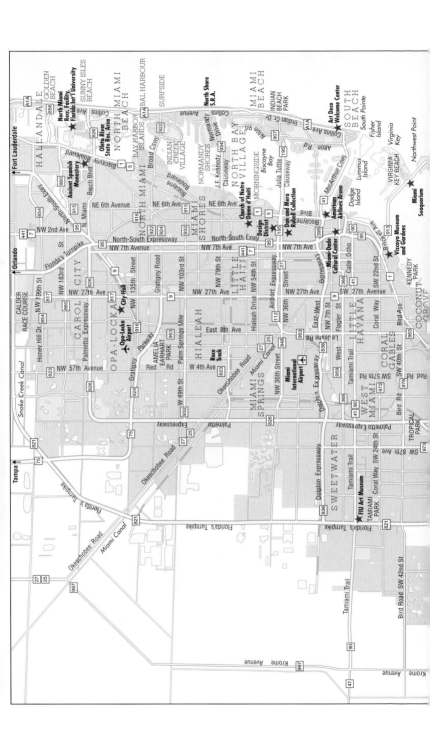

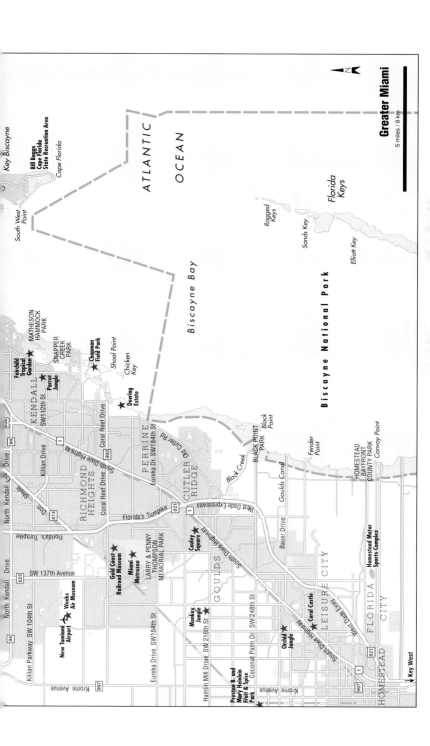

Greater Miami

5 miles / 8 km

N

ATLANTIC OCEAN

Key Biscayne

Bill Baggs Cape Florida State Recreation Area

Cape Florida

South West Point

Biscayne Bay

Florida Keys

Ragged Keys

Sands Key

Elliott Key

Biscayne National Park

MATHESON HAMMOCK PARK

Fairchild Tropical Garden

Parrot Jungle

SNAPPER CREEK PARK

Chapman Field Park

Shoal Point

Chicken Key

KENDALL

SW 112th St.

Deering Estate

SW 104th St

North Kendall Drive

SW 137th Avenue

North Kendall Drive

805

SW 137th Avenue

Killian Parkway SW 104th St

94

New Tamiami Airport

Weeks Air Museum

Krome Avenue

997

Killian Drive

South Dixie Highway

1

94

Don Shula

874

Florida's Turnpike

Coral Reef Drive

Coral Reef Drive

RICHMOND HEIGHTS

Killian Drive

992

Coral Reef Drive

PERRINE

Eureka Dr. SW184th St

CUTLER RIDGE

Old Cutler Rd

Black Creek

BLACK POINT PARK

Black Point

Fender Point

HOMESTEAD BAYFRONT COUNTY PARK

Convoy Point

Goulds Canal

Florida's Turnpike

West Dade Expressway

821

1

Cauley Square

Gold Coast Railroad Museum

Miami Metrozoo

LARRY & PENNY THOMPSON MEMORIAL PARK

GOULDS

Bauer Drive

South Dixie Highway

Monkey Jungle

Eureka Drive SW184th St

SW 216th St

Coral Castle

LEISURE CITY

Hainlin Mill Drive SW 216th St

Orchid Jungle

Coconut Palm Dr. SW 248th St

West Dade Hwy.

HOMESTEAD MOTOR SPORTS COMPLEX

Preston B. and Mary Heinlein Fruit & Spice Park

Krome Avenue

997

South Dixie Highway

821

1

FLORIDA CITY

HOMESTEAD CITY

Key West

Orientation

The state of Florida, stretching from Key West in the south to the border with Alabama in the northwest, encompasses a much larger area than many tourists imagine, and traveling by car is highly recommended. The following tour selections assume that you will have your own transportation. If you are staying in Florida for only one week, it is unlikely that you will be able to take in all the itineraries suggested; you might have to concentrate on just two or three destinations. Either way, this guide covers world-famous sites and offbeat destinations and attractions that visitors often overlook.

The five regions covered – Orlando, Tampa/St Petersburg, St Augustine, Miami/Ft Lauderdale, and the Florida Keys – are the most popular tourist areas in Florida. They each have unique features and differ greatly in character. You can easily spend three to four days in each area without getting bored. Driving times between the regions depend on the routes taken and whether you want to ramble leisurely or concentrate on getting from point A to point B. Travel times between the regions are as follows:

- Orlando – St Augustine: 2 hours
- Orlando – Tampa: 1½ hours
- Tampa – Miami: 4 hours
- Miami – Key West: 3 hours.

The suggested itineraries start in the center of Florida, then head toward the west coast, cross over to the southeast, and conclude in the southern-most portion of the state. Study the itineraries before you set off, pick the places that you would most like to visit, then organize a vacation accordingly.

Beginning in Orlando

There was a time, pre-Disney, when Orlando was no more than a small patch of commerce set amidst the extensive orange groves of central Florida. Things changed drastically following the Florida debut of a certain Mickey Mouse in 1971. Tourists, from elsewhere in the United States and from abroad, began arriving in unprecedented numbers, and in the years that followed dozens of other major attractions opened their gates to the public. Orlando's small-town atmosphere was consigned to the past. Today the Orlando area is said to be the most-visited commercial tourist destination in the world, and in the heart of it all is the city itself. You might be surprised to find that Orlando is a beautiful metropolis that, reflecting the past and the future, features a delightful blend of stately old homes and modern skyscrapers.

Left: Tigger, Disney World. **Right:** entertaining at Rosie O'Grady's Good Time Emporium

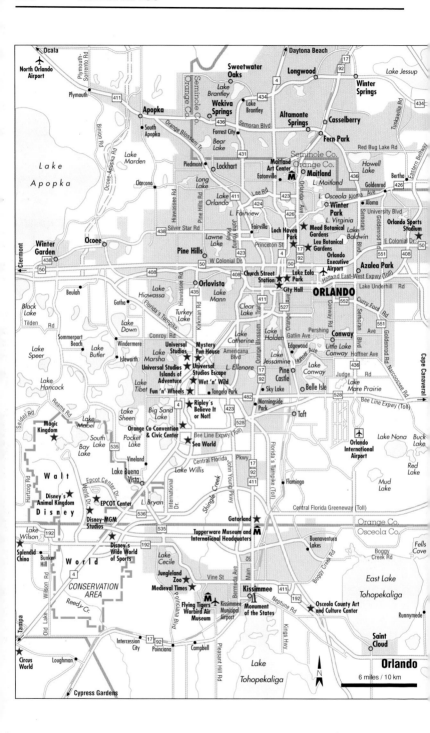

Orlando

6 miles / 10 km

1. THE CITY OF ORLANDO *(see map, p22)*

A day tour of the city of Orlando offers a glimpse of central Floridian life. Take a morning trip to the museum complex at Loch Haven Park or to the lush Leu Gardens, followed by a classic American lunch and some late-afternoon entertainment at Church Street Station.

The Orlando area's population has almost reached the one-million figure, yet the downtown area has maintained an old-fashioned, pastoral atmosphere. In the center of the city, Lake Eola Park is a peaceful spread of land surrounded by Mediterranean -style homes with jogging trails and bicycle paths. Locals take morning walks, afternoon picnics, and paddleboat rides here. In the evenings, horse-drawn carriages take passengers for a gentle spin around the grounds.

To the north of Orlando's downtown district, off Mills Avenue, **Loch Haven Park** is an expanse of red-brick pathways and moss-draped oak trees. In the park are four museums. The **Orange County Historical Museum** (Tues–Fri 10am–4pm, Sat, Sun 1–5pm), has a substantial collection of exhibits on local history. The **Orlando Science Center** (Mon–Thur 9am–5pm, Fri 9am–9pm, Sat noon–9pm, Sun noon–5pm) offers a variety of educational science exhibits and a planetarium. **Fire Station No. 3** (Tues–Fri 10am–4pm, Sat, Sun 1–5pm) dates back to 1926 and is the city's oldest standing fire station. This is the place to see antique fire-fighting equipment and displays of related memorabilia. Art lovers will enjoy the **Orlando Fine Arts Museum** (Tues–Fri 10am–5pm, Sat, Sun 1–5pm), which houses a sophisticated collection of both classic and contemporary art. Most museums charge a small entrance fee, but parking in Loch Haven Park is free.

Not far from the park, the **Maitland Art Center** (Mon–Fri 10am–4pm, Sat, Sun 1–5pm) on West Packwood Avenue was built in the 1930s by the artist Andre Smith as a winter retreat for fellow artists and kindred free-spirit types. A lush, green suburban community surrounded by manicured gardens and public-use courtyards, the Maitland Center incorporates studios and living quarters alike. The studios are full of Aztec and Mayan Indian decorations.

A horticultural showpiece

If you would rather spend your morning outdoors, drive a few miles west of the downtown area on North Forest Avenue until you see the signpost for **Leu Botanical Gardens** (Tues–Sat 10am–4pm, Sun, Mon 1–4pm). This 56-acre (23-hectare) park is full of roses, camellias, palms, and azaleas. Once a private estate, the gardens were transformed into a horticultural showpiece and educational center. Today the peaceful grounds evoke an

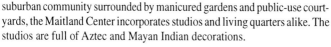

Right: water fun at Orlando's EPCOT Center

atmosphere redolent of a Zen retreat. Features include an orchid conservatory, a formal European-style rose garden, a native wetland garden, a ravine and waterfalls, and a cactus collection. The house is now a museum that hosts lectures on subjects such as herbal wines, and spice growing.

Rosie O'Grady and Apple Annie

When you're ready for lunch, drive toward the downtown area south of Lake Eola Park, and find a parking space in one of the public lots near Church Street. On Church Street you can't miss the city's liveliest and most popular attraction. **Church Street Station** (daily 11am–2am) is a dazzling emporium of stores, shows, restaurants, bars, and dance halls. Although the admission charge is a bit expensive, it covers live entertainment and entrance to all the attractions. Once you get into the mood of the place, you will probably want to stay for the evening floor shows. Opened in the 1970s by an adventurous biplane pilot, Church Street Station has grown from the

small and funky **Rosie O'Grady's Good Time Emporium** (which still exists) to become a massive entertainment complex. Typical features include high-kicking dancing girls, ragtime music, hearty food, generously poured drinks, and Victorian antiques.

For lunch, try the emporium's **Cheyenne Barbecue Restaurant**. Its decor – solid oak beams that once supported the roof of an old barn, and country & western artwork – is oddly complemented by ornate stained glass. The menu features barbecue beef ribs, buffalo burgers, hickory-smoked brisket, and huge steins of beer.

Another interesting lunch spot in Rosie O'Grady's is **Apple Annie's Courtyard**. Here an eclectic decor mixes antiques from 19th-century New Orleans and 18th-century Vienna with old English pub tables. Along with the hearty Americana food, Annie's serves up folk and blues music.

After eating, take a walk and explore: **Phineas Phogg's Balloon Works**, Church Street Station's popular disco/dance club-cum-ballooning museum, has artifacts from historic balloon flights; the **Cheyenne Saloon and Opera House** is a recreation of a Western-style saloon with wooden Indians and an antique gun collection; the **Church Street Railroad Depot** consists of an antique railroad car surrounded by an assortment of pushcart vendors.

Another fun spot for a late-afternoon visit is the **Orchid Garden Ballroom**. Though the building is a Victorian-style affair, its ballroom is a shrine to rock and roll, from the 1950s up to the 1990s. Alternatively, you could try the **Exchange Shopping Emporium**, a rambling collection of one-of-a-kind stores selling 10-gallon cowboy hats, leather boots with spurs, silver and turquoise belt buckles, suede jackets, and fancy pocket knives.

Above: high-kicking dancing girls at Rosie O'Grady's Good Time Emporium

2. WALT DISNEY WORLD *(see map, p22)*

A visit to Florida's best-loved attraction.

The granddaddy of all Florida theme parks, **Walt Disney World** lies about 20 miles (32km) south of Orlando in Lake Buena Vista off I-4. From the interstate highway three exits lead into the 27,000-acre (11,000-ha) resort. The first leads to the Disney hotel complex, the second to the EPCOT Center, and the third to the Magic Kingdom and Disney-MGM Studios. Each parking lot is as big as a small town; a monorail makes getting around easy.

Opening Times

Walt Disney World is open 365 days a year, but hours vary according to the time of year and holiday schedules. All attractions officially open at 9am, but the gates open at 8am. Closing times vary from 6pm to 10pm, depending on the attraction. For operating hours and general information on all of the attractions call 407-934 7639 or 1-800-828-0228. The busiest days of the week are Mon, Tues and Wed; the least crowded are Fri and Sun. Disney is famous for its crowd control – be prepared for long, but fast-moving lines. Cameras, baby carriages, and wheelchairs are available for rent, as are lockers in which you can store bags that you don't want to carry.

Tickets and Costs

For admission purposes, anyone over 10 is considered an adult, children are those between 3 and 9, and toddlers get in free of charge. Tickets take the form of one-day, four-day, five-day, and six-day passes, and include admission to all

Above: Mickey and friends take flight
Left: hiding out at Donald Duck's place

exhibits and rides. One-day tickets entitle you to enter one of the three venues; the others grant you entrance to all of the attractions, and unlimited use of the on-site transportation system. Some theme parks within the venues offer separate, single-day admission rates. Tickets can be purchased at the attractions' entrance booths, from several Orlando area hotels, and from Orlando's airport. If you need to leave one of the venues and plan on returning the same day, you are obliged to have your hand stamped. A day at Walt Disney World is expensive – count on spending at least $65 per adult and $55 per child for entrance costs and meals, and a few dollars for parking your car.

The Magic Kingdom

The **Magic Kingdom** is where you'll find most of the Mickey Mouse action. Set in almost 100 acres (40 ha), this enchanting fantasyland consists of a maze of some 50 separate attractions and dozens of restaurants and stores. The entrance leads to **Main Street**, **USA**, a happy, wholesome, life-sized model of small-town America, complete with a city hall, town square, and horse-drawn trolleys. The **Main Street Cinema** screens vintage Disney cartoons. After Main Street you reach the Magic Kingdom's focal point, **Cinderella Castle**, which, with its majestic spires, was designed to resemble King Ludwig's castle in Bavaria. At the castle's entrance, a series of mosaic murals relate the tale of the poor little cinder girl and her fairy godmother. Although there's no dungeon beneath the castle, there is a secret labyrinth of service tunnels through which the tons of trash produced by the kingdom are funneled.

Over the bridge on the castle's west side is **Adventureland**, a series of exotic attractions and rides including **Pirates of the Caribbean** (cruise through a simulated pirate raid), and **Swiss Family Treehouse**. Nearby is **Frontierland**, a re-creation of the American frontier (1770s–1880s) with a shooting arcade, jail, cemetery, and a terrifying rollercoaster ride.

Liberty Square has the spooky **Haunted Mansion**, the **Liberty Square Riverboat** rides, and the **Hall of Presidents** – a rather dry historical attraction. **Fantasyland**, on the east side of Cinderella Castle, features a collection of rides inspired by classic children's stories – the **Mad Tea Party**, **Dumbo the Flying Elephant**, and **Peter Pan's Flight**. Young children in particular love Fantasyland. At **Mickey Mouse at Starland** you can visit **Duckburg** and have your picture taken at Mickey's house. For entertainment of a more thrilling variety, try **Space Mountain** in the recently revamped

Tomorrowland. This rollercoaster takes you, in the dark, on a space-age journey through a simulated galaxy of shooting stars. The Astro Orbitor and The Timekeeper are alternative options for exciting rides here.

EPCOT Center

The **EPCOT Center** is an acronym for Experimental Prototype Community of Tomorrow, and represents the realization of Walter Elias Disney's deathbed dream. Divided into two distinct attractions, Future World and the World Showcase, it is a display of modern technology and a permanent world fair.

The **Future World** showcase occupies the southern half of the 260-acre (105-ha) park. Themes here include energy, communications, transportation, oceanography, and agriculture. The attractions have an educational purpose, though this can be lost under the promotional messages of the corporate giants that sponsor the exhibits. The 17-story silver geosphere that is **Spaceship Earth** transports you on a historic journey from the days of Cro-Magnon man right up to the present. **Horizons** is a display of futuristic lifestyles complete with robots and space cities, **The Living Seas** examines all aspects of marine life, and **Wonders of Life** looks at all aspects of the human body.

Across the 40-acre (16-ha) lagoon from Future World you will find the **World Showcase**, a promenade of pavilions dedicated to the history, art, music, and food of cultures throughout the world. France, Morocco, Japan, Italy, Germany, Norway, Canada, the United Kingdom, Mexico, China, and of course the US are all represented in individual pavilions. Natives from these countries serve as hosts, and the gift shops sell indigenous crafts. The displays are on the lines of a Parisian café, a Munich-style beer hall, and an Aztec-inspired Mexican pyramid and a Moroccan bazaar.

Disney-MGM Studios

Disney-MGM Studios is a working television and film studio as well as a theme park. The studio's **Backstage Studio Tour** and **Animation Tour** are ideal for film buffs who want behind-the-scenes lessons in special effects, scenery and sound production, and costuming. The **Great Movie Ride** is an animated tour through re-created movie sets: see John Wayne on horseback, Gene Kelly singing in the rain, Tarzan swinging through the jungle, Dorothy and friends dancing down the Yellow Brick Road, and the tearful farewell scene from *Casablanca*. The **Twilight Zone Tower of Terror** has become one of the most exciting and popular scare rides – the elevator 'crashes' with all aboard. Inspired by George Lucas's *Star Wars*, **Star Tours** is a rollicking tour through outer space. Be warned, however, that this is a rough ride and is not recommended for those who suffer back problems, heart conditions, or motion sickness.

Left: showing no fear on a rollercoaster ride at Tomorrowland's Space Mountain
Right: the EPCOT Center's unmistakable geosphere

3. OTHER THEME PARKS *(see map, p22)*

If you have a spare day and are still in the mood for make-believe, you might consider a day at one of the many other attractions in the area.

One of the newest is **Universal Studios Florida** (daily 9am–6pm, entrance 1½ miles/3km north of I-4 on Kirkman Road), a television and film center similar to the Disney-MGM Studios, and with comparable admission fees. This is the largest non-Hollywood studio in the country and many consider its attractions superior to those at Disney. Some 40 sets include the bustling sidewalks of New York City, San Francisco's Fisherman's Wharf, a charming New England village, and the garden of Allah. This is the place to survive an attack by King Kong, feel the violent rumble of an earthquake, sail past the 24-ft (7.3-meter) killer shark from *Jaws*, and witness the terrifying shower scene from Alfred Hitchcock's *Psycho*. You can also take a screen test and star in your own *Star Trek* video, meet the friendly alien ET, and take a lesson in the techniques of horror movie make-up. After an entertaining day at Universal Studios, check out the **Hard Rock Café** on the studio premises. This outlet of the worldwide chain known for its rock music memorabilia serves excellent cheeseburgers and other American favorites.

Simulated Surfing Lagoon

Wet 'n' Wild (Jun–Sept: daily 9am–9pm; Oct–May: 10am–5pm; closed Jan–mid-Feb) on International Drive near Universal Studios, is a massive, 25-acre (10-ha) water theme park with any number of water slides, flumes, floats, and plunges. You can spend a day here in your bathing suit, and you don't have to be an adept swimmer. The water depths never exceed standing height and there are always lifeguards on duty. You can ride 4-ft (one meter-plus) waves in a simulated surfing lagoon, raft through white-water rapids, free-fall down a 250-ft (75-meter) slide, and water-ski on a knee board or inner tube around a freshwater lake. Admission fees are moderate and there are plenty of food kiosks from which you can create your own picnic.

Above: the *Beetlejuice* set at Universal Studios Florida

Just south of Wet 'n' Wild at the intersection of I-4 and the Bee Line Expressway is **Sea World** (daily 9am–7pm), the world's largest marine park. Sea World is on a par with Walt Disney World when it comes to putting on an elaborate show. Admission fees are moderate and the well-organized park offers all the amenities a family might need. Although situated an hour's drive from the nearest stretch of coast, Sea World makes you feel as if you are in the middle of the Atlantic Ocean.

Sea World's biggest star, in more ways than one, is Shamu the Killer Whale, who weighs in at 5,000lbs (2,260kg). She might be a killer by name but Shamu's audience-pleasing tricks are of the jumps, flips, and kisses variety. Other popular performers include sea lions, penguins, dolphins, otters, and a gregarious walrus. One of Sea World's more educational exhibits is the shark tank, at which you can learn all about these deadly creatures and watch as they indulge in a bloody feeding frenzy. Check out a feeding pool populated by seals that will eat herrings virtually from your hand or, if you are looking for something more sophisticated, take a trip in a research submarine. In the evenings Sea World hosts a Polynesian-style luau dinner show complete with hula dancers and fire jugglers.

In contrast with the theme parks, **Cypress Gardens** (daily 9am–6pm) is one of the oldest attractions in the state. Located in the town of **Winter Haven**, a 40-minute drive south of Walt Disney World, off I-4, the gardens were founded during the Depression. The park's 223 acres (90 ha) form one of the world's lushest botanical gardens and include more than 8,000 species of flowers and plants. The gardens are known for their world-champion water-skiing events, synchronized swimmers, and parrot and alligator shows.

International Oddities

Like the 20 other Ripley's in cities around the world, **Ripley's Believe It Or Not!** museum (daily 10am–midnight) on International Drive is dedicated to the preservation of oddities and curiosities. Here you can see a 20-ft (6-meter) segment of the Berlin Wall, a gruesome torture gallery, and a 20-ft (6-meter) mural portrait of Van Gogh made from 3,000 postcards.

Fun 'n' Wheels (Sand Lake Road; Mon–Fri 6–11pm, Sat, Sun 10am–11pm), another Orlando attraction near International Drive, is the perfect park for adults who love four-wheel playthings. Here you can ride in bumper cars and go-carts, sail on boats, and play miniature golf. Fun 'n' Wheels is a simple but entertaining place where you pay only for the rides you take and nothing for admission. The **Mystery Fun House** (daily 10am–11pm), on Major Drive in Orlando, appeals to horror movie fans. Its mansion is full of moving floors, magic mirrors, and monsters that jump out of closets and frighten the living daylights out of visitors.

The **Tupperware Museum and International Headquarters** (Mon–Fri 9am–4pm) on US 441 on the south side of Orlando is a good example

Right: riding the dolphin at Wet 'n' Wild

of the only-in-Florida genre of attractions. This museum is dedicated to those American-made, plastic food containers that have made the lives of hard-pressed homemakers just a little easier. The Tupperware headquarters offers a 25-minute guided tour that explains the history of food storage from early civilizations to the present day. The collection includes a food container that dates back to 4000BC, and the **Museum of Dishes** occupies an entire wing. Admission is free. Even if Tupperware doesn't strike you as the most fascinating subject in the world, the museum could prove to be a surprisingly refreshing diversion on a rainy day.

4. KISSIMMEE *(see map, p22)*

A day trip south of Orlando to the old-time Florida town of Kissimmee.

By this stage you might conceivably have had enough of the seemingly ubiquitous theme-park scene. If this is the case, and you would like to escape for a day of reality, consider taking a drive south of Orlando to Kissimmee, wedged between the Florida Turnpike and I-4. Kissimmee is still a small place with quaint old homes, towering 100-year-old oak trees, and residents of the courteous old-school who still say 'good morning' to strangers. Kissimmee was once a bustling, thriving place with a busy station on the Seaboard Railroad line. Small hotels attracted winter travelers, and saloons allowed cowboys to ride up on their horses for a shot of red-eye. All this came to an end with the advent of the state's highway system. Kissimmee fell into hard times, from which it has never fully recovered.

The Rodeo Crowd

Kissimmee is the home of the **Florida Cattlemen's Association**, and this is where many of the state's livestock shows and (usually on Wednesdays) cattle auctions take place. Kissimmee is also a social center for the state's hard-working ranch hands and for the cowboys who form the rodeo crowd. The town's annual **Silver Spurs Rodeo** – which is one of the country's

leading 25 rodeos – takes place in February and July. For information about the Silver Spurs or other rodeos in the area call 407-847 5118.

The majority of Kissimmee's authentic old buildings were torn down several decades ago but, in an attempt to re-create the history of this part of Florida, Kissimmee's development council decided to create what it calls the **Old Town** district. A synthetic, manufactured enclave that was designed to resemble a 19th-century city, Old Town has the appearance and atmosphere of a rustic, frontier metropolis. The streets are paved with bricks and there are several re-created antique shops. A good lunch option in Kissimmee is **People's Place** on Broadway. Housed in a former blacksmith stable, it offers a bargain-priced hot buffet prepared by students attending a nearby culinary school. The menus vary daily.

Opposite the railroad station near the downtown district is Lake Front Park, which hosts concerts and art shows. The **Monument of the States** in the park is a 50-ft (15-meter) high statue made of 1,500 stones from all 50 states and from 21 other countries. A garish conglomerate of marble, coral, platinum, agate, and slate, the monument was designed by a local tourist club during World War II to represent their hope for world unity.

Alligators and Aircraft

Though it is off the tourist-beaten track, Kissimmee is not immune to the lure of the visitor's dollar. The **Gatorland Zoo** (daily; Sept–May: 8am–6pm; June–Aug: 8am–8pm) on Orange Blossom Trail confirms the abundance of these mean-looking reptiles, which were once an endangered species in Florida. More than 4,000 alligators sleep in the sun beside a muddy lake, and at feeding time jump out of the water to snap at dead chickens dangling from an overhead line. The zoo features crocodiles, snakes, birds, and alligator-wrestling shows.

The **Flying Tigers Warbird Air Museum** (daily 9am–6pm), on Hoagland Boulevard, houses one of the finest collections of antique aircraft and aviation artifacts in the US. A working museum with restoration projects underway, the Warbird Museum charges a small admission fee that is worth it for the informative guided tour.

One of the most unusual attractions to be spawned by Mickey Mouse and friends is **Splendid China** (daily from 9.30am), which is set in a 76-acre (31-ha) park near Kissimmee. More than 60 of China's cultural, historical and natural sites are re-created in miniature, to scale (the Great Wall model is 2,600ft/7,920 meters long). There are gift shops, of course, and live entertainment, including jugglers, dancers, acrobats and martial artists.

Left: a Florida Cattlemen's Association member. **Above:** a Gatorland resident
Right: the Kennedy Space Center includes exhibits about the 1969 moon landing

5. KENNEDY SPACE CENTER *(see pullout map)*

The Kennedy Space Center is situated about an hour's drive east of Orlando via the Bee Line Expressway and State Road 407. It is well worth a day trip.

Formerly called Cape Canaveral, the **Kennedy Space Center** on Merrit Island is the launchpad for the US's space shuttle. The center sprawls across 110,000 acres (45,000 ha) of heavily guarded, in some places top-secret, grounds where the latest in space technology is created. The center's aim, according to the National Aeronautics and Space Administration, is to carry out the peaceful exploration of outer space and the solar system through communications satellites and automated spacecraft. Much of the surrounding land has been declared a National Wildlife Preserve and is part of the **Canaveral National Seashore**. A vast eco-system of plant life, birds, fish, alligators, wild pigs, deer, and raccoons coexists in the mudflats and waterways.

Spaceport USA (daily 9am–dusk, closed Christmas; free, but charge for bus tour into Kennedy Space Center), a mile from the center, attracts over three million visitors a year. Its two-hour bus tour stops at the shuttle launch pads and the Saturn V Moon Rocket. You can walk through a simulated space station at the **Satellites and You** exhibit.

At **Exploration Station** children can try on space suits and test their skills in outer space navigation. Other points of interest include the **Astronauts Hall of Fame** and the **Planetarium**. The **Astronauts Memorial** honors the 15 American astronauts who lost their lives in the line of duty. An array of exhibits in the grounds includes moon rocks, lunar rovers, telescopes, satellites, and rockets. For lunch, you can visit the Spaceport USA cafeteria.

During an actual launch, Spaceport USA is closed to the public, but it usually opens a few hours later. The launch schedule is irregular, so for

Above: the Kennedy Space Center is the launchpad for the American space shuttle

upcoming dates and general information call 321-867 4636. Viewing a live blast-off can be a thrilling sensation; you need not be at the center – the rockets can be seen and felt from miles away. The best viewing spots are at Jetty Park in Cocoa Beach just south of the center, and on Highway A1A along the Indian River. It takes about five hours to explore the center, and foreign language audio tours are available. School groups take trips to the center during the week; weekends are less crowded.

6. ST AUGUSTINE   *(see map, p34)*

A full day spent exploring historic St Augustine, taking in the Old Town, and Castillo de San Marcos, followed by dinner on St Augustine Beach.

Situated on the state's northeast coast, St Augustine is a 2½-hour drive from Orlando. From I-95, exits to the city are clearly marked by highway signs. The closest airport is in Jacksonville, about an hour's drive to the north.

St Augustine is the oldest continuously occupied city in the USA. Founded on the feast day of St Augustine in 1565 by Spain's Pedro Menendez de Aviles, St Augustine was an established European outpost when the first Pilgrims landed at Plymouth Rock about 50 years later. For its first 150 years, the Spanish stronghold endured countless battles with Native Americans, the British, and ruthless pirates. In 1702 much of St Augustine was ravaged by fire, but it was quickly reconstructed, and today the 'Nation's Oldest City' is filled with narrow brick-lined roads, horse-drawn carriages, ancient oak trees, a grand old fort, shady courtyards, and restored Spanish colonial architecture.

The **St Augustine Visitor Information Center** (daily 8.30am–7.30pm) at 10 Castillo Drive is helpful, as is the tourist information booth in Government House (daily 9am–6pm) on King Street. Several trolley companies offer a seven-mile city tour, and horse-drawn carriages run from locations around town. The Visitor Information Center sells tickets for these tours, whose prices include admission fees to historic properties. Most of the historic attractions have full-time tour guides, dressed in period costumes, to answer visitors's questions.

The Spanish Quarter Village

Dating back to the 18th century, two towering stone columns form the **City Gate** on George Street, which serves as the main entrance to **Old Town**, the city's historic district. Filled with antique and craft stores, and art galleries, St. George Street is a pedestrian thoroughfare that bustles with activity, day and night. At the end of the street is the **Spanish Quarter Village**, a collection of historic buildings and attractions. Built in the mid-18th century out of native cypress and red cedar wood, the **Oldest Wooden Schoolhouse** on St George Street has a replica of its original classroom complete with a dungeon for naughty students. It is said to be the oldest wooden

Right: looking out from the Oldest Store Museum

schoolhouse still standing in the US. Also on St. George is the **Pena-Peck House**. One of the finest early Spanish colonial homes in the city, it is filled with period antiques and art, and has been restored to its original condition.

Lastly, St George Street is the **Bunnery Bakery and Café**, a great place to stop for a late morning snack of stuffed croissants, home-made soups, and iced cappuccinos.

Reminder of a Gilded Age

Nearby on King Street, which intersects with George Street, are several points of interest. The old Alcazar Hotel houses the **Lightner Museum** (daily 9am–5pm), an impressive reminder of Florida's Gilded Age. A grand Spanish-Moorish building with an open center courtyard, it contains a collection of fine Victorian antiques, sculptures, furniture, paintings, Tiffany glass, musical instruments, and toys. It also has a science wing housing minerals and gems, seashells, stuffed birds, steam engine models, Native American artifacts, and an authentic Egyptian mummy.

Opposite the Lightner you will find **Flagler College**, named in honor of railroad magnate Henry Flagler, who once owned a luxury hotel in the building. During the long summer vacation, tourists are welcomed into the college to view its historic art collection. Also on King Street is **Zorayda Castle**. A former private residence, it was built in 1883 and designed to

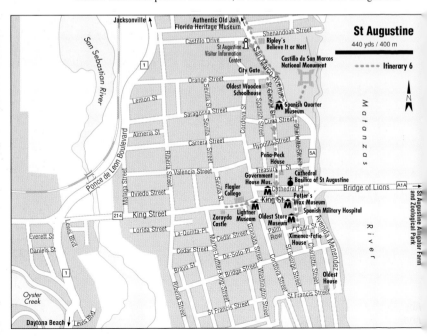

resemble the incredible Alhambra Palace in Granada, Spain. Today the castle contains a wonderful collection of Oriental art and artifacts.

About three blocks away from Zorayda Castle on Avile Street is the **Ximenez-Fatio House**. The former home of a wealthy Spanish merchant, this 1797 structure served as a boarding house for Florida land developers and travelers, and is now an antiques-filled museum run by the National Society of Colonial Dames. Also on Avile Street is the **Spanish Military Hospital**, a reconstructed clapboard structure that is now a museum filled with antique operating tables, apothecary jars, surgical instruments, a herbarium, and a spartan sick ward that treated Spanish soldiers toward the end of the 18th century. A block away on Artillery Lane is the **Oldest Store Museum**. From 1835 to 1960, this rustic site housed the C & F Hamblen General Store. Today its 100,000-plus exhibits, drawn from items once sold here include canned soups, commercial soaps, chewing tobacco, medicines, pickle barrels, box cameras, horse saddles, butter churns, spinning wheels, high-button shoes, straw bonnets, and bathing suits.

About six blocks from Avile Street, on the banks of the Matanzas River near San Marco Avenue, is one of the most visited attractions in the St Augustine area, **Castillo de San Marcos National Monument** (daily 8.45am– 4.45pm). Built between 1672 and 1695, San Marcos is the largest and best preserved Spanish fort in the US. Complete with a double drawbridge that spans a 40-ft (12-meter) dry moat, it is an impressive symmetrical fortress with diamond shaped bastions, sentry towers, a vaulted powder magazine, tidal-flush sewage system, watchtower, gun deck, shot furnace, chapel, kitchen, and lock-tight prison. Constructed out of coquina rock, a natural sedimentary limestone formed by compressed seashells and coral pieces, San Marcos withstood countless attacks by the British in the 18th century while it guarded the Spanish fleets before they set sail for Europe. In 1821, when the US gained possession of Florida, it was renamed Fort Marion, and for a while it served as a military storage center and prison.

Declared a US National Monument in 1924, it houses exhibits and documents about the city's history. There are guided tours several times a day.

Weird and Wonderful

A block away from the fortress and also on San Marcos Avenue is one of the few gratuitously commercial tourist spots in the Old Town district. Set in an authentic 1887 Moorish Revival home, **Ripley's Believe It Or Not!** (daily 9am–10pm) contains a circus-like collection of bizarre knick-knacks from around the world including a voodoo doll supposedly once owned and used by 'Papa Doc' Duvalier, the former dictator of Haiti.

About eight blocks to the north on San Marco Avenue is the **Authentic Old Jail**. Although it is small in size, this 1890 brick structure served as a working jail for the St Augustine community up until 1953. While it was

Above Left: St Augustine is full of living re-creations of the city's history
Above: a statue of Henry Flagler outside the college named for him

in operation as a jail, the local sheriff and his family lived above the felons on the second floor. Today's museum has restored prison cells, gallows, and a solitary-confinement pen. Next door to the jail, the **Florida Heritage Museum** has a collection that spans 400 years of Florida history, including a replica of a Spanish galleon, guns, cannons, gold and silver bars, artifacts from the Civil War and the Florida Seminole Wars, toys, dolls, clothing, and jewelry salvaged from sunken treasure ships.

An Old Florida Tourist Haunt

Following a day's exploration of the city's historic side, you might take a trip to St Augustine Beach, where you will find some pure Florida kitsch. Cross the Bridge of Lions which leads to Anastasia Avenue and, in particular, the **St Augustine Alligator Farm and Zoological Park** (daily 9am–6pm). Opened in 1893, this Old Florida tourist haunt heralds itself as 'The World's Original Alligator Attraction.' A meandering property of lush ponds and thick vegetation, the farm features a petting zoo with miniature horses, pygmy goats, sheep, pigs, and deer. There are also flocks of geese, swans, lizards, snakes, turtles, monkeys, skinks, and exotic birds. The highlight is the collection of over 1,000 reptiles, including alligators, crocodiles, caimans, and gavials. Crocodile feedings and alligator-wrestling shows add a little zest.

Continue on Anastasia Avenue to St Augustine Beach, a quiet oceanfront town with a 4 mile (7km) stretch of sand. The main drag here is A1A, a north–south road parallel to the ocean. The **Oasis Deck and Restaurant** on A1A South is one of the area's most popular eateries and a great place to wind up the day. The action starts at happy hour (4–7pm). Friendly with an English pub atmosphere, the Oasis serves hefty portions of grilled fish, fried clams, steamed shrimp, spicy chili, and good burgers.

Above: the most natural attraction
Left: Castillo de San Marcos

Tampa & St Petersburg

Though a long spell of sunshine is nothing to brag about in Florida, the state's central west coast takes the prize when it comes to blue skies. Listed in the *Guinness Book of World Records* for the longest-ever run of consecutive sunny days – from February 9, 1967 to March 17, 1969 – the 25-mile (40 km) stretch of soft-sand beaches known as the Suncoast consistently lives up to the reputation suggested by its name.

Located about 75 miles (120km) southwest of Orlando, off Route 4, the twin cites of Tampa and St Petersburg are separated by the pretty, but polluted, Tampa Bay. Driving from the north or the south, the cities can be reached from I-75. One of the fastest growing regions in America, the urban area has a combined population of more than two million. It also serves as the spring training-ground for several American major-league baseball teams, whose players get in shape and practise their technique at area stadiums.

7. TAMPA *(see map, p38)*

A full day spent exploring Tampa, taking in the best museums, followed by lunch on Harbor Island and a trip to the Latin-flavored Ybor City.

The city of **Tampa**, in Hillsborough County, is a dynamic metropolis that has a sophisticated and modern downtown center, and an ethnically rich historic quarter. A good way to plan a day tour of the city is to concentrate on the downtown area in the morning, perhaps picking a museum or two of interest, and then heading to Ybor City for a late-afternoon walk and dinner at a Cuban restaurant. Traffic in the downtown area is dense and driving can be tense. Once you arrive, and have decided which spots you want to visit, leave your car at one of the many public parking lots and walk through the city.

The heart of the downtown business district lies on the banks of the **River Hillsborough**, not far from the **Port of Tampa**. There are several points of interest within a few square miles. In walking distance from the **University of Tampa** campus, the **Henry B Plant Museum** (Tues–Sat 10am–4pm, Sun noon–4pm) on West Kennedy Boulevard is housed in a former hotel. Henry B Plant was a railroad tycoon who played a key role in the development of Tampa in the mid-19th century. The five-story museum once featured a casino, two grand ballrooms, and an indoor swimming-pool. Today, it serves as a

Above: on the boardwalk, Tampa

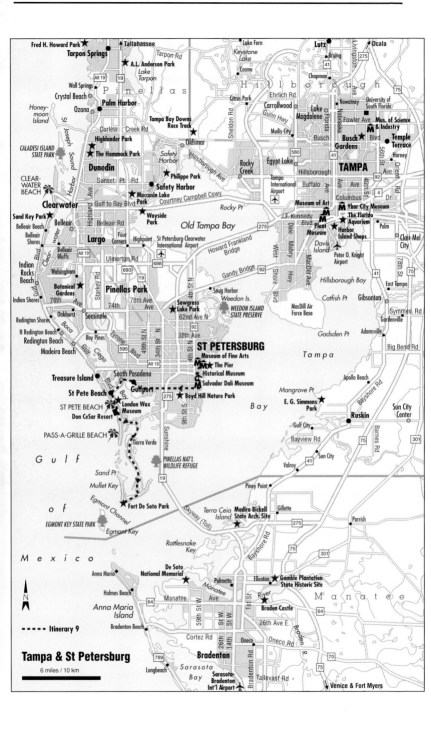

Tampa & St Petersburg

6 miles / 10 km

- - - - - Itinerary 9

N

showcase for Plant's collection of Victorian art, furniture, and fashion items. Donations to the museum are invited.

A short walk across the river on Doyle Carlton Drive leads to the **Tampa Museum of Art** (Mon, Tues, Thur–Sat 10am–5pm, Wed 10am–9pm, Sun 1–5pm; small entrance fee), one of Florida's best art museums. The museum presents 15 changing exhibits yearly and has a collection of more than 7,000 art works that include classic Greek and Roman antiquities, Egyptian artifacts and modern American art. The museum can easily take up to an hour or two.

A few blocks away, at 711 on the pedestrian-only Franklin Street Mall, one of the country's few remaining grand old single-screen movie theaters, **The Tampa Theater** (tel: 813-274 8981) screens foreign and art movies on a weekly basis, usually at weekends. This theater still has its tall pillars, curved box seats, a balcony, and an organ that rises from the basement – all under a ceiling of painted clouds and twinkling stars. Built in 1926, the theater was beautifully restored in Florida-Mediterranean style.

From Science to Fish

If you're not interested in the art museum, your morning might be better spent at the **Museum of Science and Industry** (Sun–Thur 9am–5pm, Fri, Sat 9am–7pm) at the north end of the city on East Fowler Avenue. One of the largest science centers in the southeast, the museum has a planetarium, a butterfly garden, and exhibits dedicated to scientific inventions. Children who pour their souls into the creation of sixth-grade science projects adore it.

Alternatively, one of Tampa's lesser known treasures is **The Florida Aquarium** (daily 9am–6pm) at 701 Channelside Drive, right on the city's busy waterfront. The newest West Coast attraction, the aquarium features more than 4,300 varieties of fish – including sharks and stingrays, and the million-gallon Coral Reefs Gallery is fascinating. When you have seen enough or lunch time rolls around, you can nip across (by car, boat, or Tampa's downtown train) to the Harbor Island shopping and restaurants complex.

After lunch, take a stroll through **Ybor City**. An ethnic enclave full of old character (and characters), Ybor City is actually a neighborhood rather than a proper city. It's located in the northwest corner of Tampa and is bounded by Columbus Drive, Fifth Avenue, Nebraska Avenue, and 22nd Street. The 110-block area is one of the three national landmark districts in Florida.

Above: riding the dolphin, Tampa Museum of Art
Right: an unusual view from the university

tampa/st.petersburg

Founded in 1886 by Don Vicente Martinez Ybor, a wealthy Cuban tobacco merchant, Ybor City attracted cigar factory workers from Key West and Cuba in the years around the turn of the 20th century. In its heyday, its 50 cigar factories employed more than 40,000 workers and was known as the 'Cigar Capital of the World.' The area was a lively business district where recent immigrants – Cubans, Spaniards, Italians, Germans, and Jews – all worked together. Although an ethnically mixed neighborhood, Ybor City's Hispanic character was, and still is, dominant. Store owners lived above their stores, talked to their neighbors from their balconies, and socialized at the many casinos and speakeasies. But the austere years of the Depression,

and the sacrifices required by World War II, hit Ybor City hard. Factories closed down and families moved away. In the following years it fell deeper and deeper into decay. Many of the buildings were demolished; lots of those that remained became squatters' homes.

Return to the Good Old Days

But Tampa was determined to bring back its beautiful historic treasure, and the seeds of an Ybor City renewal project were planted in the late 1970s. Old cigar factories were turned into shopping centers and restaurants, and much of the architecture was restored. The red-brick streets were repaired and the old gas streetlamps refurbished. Today the district appears almost as it did in the long-lost good old days, with plenty of ornate grillwork and Spanish-style architecture.

Tourists flock to its streets, as do locals who come by for drinks after work. If you arrive in time you can catch one of the free walking tours (Tues, Thur, Sat 1.30pm, tel: 813-223 1111) that depart from the **Ybor Square Visitors Center** on 14th Street. If you miss the tour, pick up a free walking-tour map at the center and wander around on your own. Next door to the visitors center is **Ybor Square** (Mon–Sat 9.30am–5.30pm, Sun noon–5.30pm), the former site of the original Ybor Cigar Factory and now a shopping center with vintage clothing boutiques, customized jewelry shops, art galleries, and Cuban grocery stores and cafés. Walk two blocks south of Ybor Square to Seventh Avenue. Here you will find **El Sol Cigars** (Mon–Sat 9am–5pm) where you can pick up a box of thick, hand-rolled Cuban cigars, and the **El Molino Coffee Shop** (Mon–Sat 9am–5pm) which sells strong Cuban coffee roasted on the premises.

Continue walking down Seventh Avenue until you come to 18th Street. To your right will be the **Italian Club**, a social center for Ybor's Italian-American community. Turn left on 18th Street and walk two blocks until you get to Ninth Avenue; here you will see the massive brick structure that houses the

Above: Ybor City pays tribute to the 'Cradle of Cuban Liberty'

Ybor City State Museum (Tues–Sat 9am–noon, 1–5pm). Formerly the Ferlita Bakery building, dating back to 1923, the museum complex includes three restored cigar workers' homes where the smell of tobacco still permeates the air. It offers a walk-through history lesson on Ybor City that is full of historic photographs and artifacts from the cigar industry.

No visit to Ybor City is complete without a robust, Spanish-style meal. The neighborhood's favorite eatery, and said to be the oldest restaurant in Florida, founded in 1905, is the **Columbia Restaurant** (daily 11am–10pm) on Seventh Avenue. The Columbia's ornate European decor, including hand-painted tiles, complements the food: the specialty is a saffron-rich paella accompanied by a salad of lettuce, ham, cheese, olives, and lots of garlic. After your meal, stop in at **Centro Ybor** (daily 10am–midnight) a few blocks away on Eighth Avenue. The newest attraction in the area, this large entertainment complex houses several restaurants and bars, shops, and a Game Works interactive video arcade designed by movie director Steven Spielberg.

8. BUSCH GARDENS *(see map, p38)*

A full-day expedition to an 'African safari' theme park.

Tampa has a lot to offer, but **Busch Gardens** (daily 9.30am–6pm, extended hours in summer) constitutes the main reason for most tourists to visit the city. Located about 8 miles (13km) northeast of downtown Tampa, just west of I-75 on exit 54, the 300-acre (120-ha) theme park is one of the best in the state. A miniature, sanitized Africa, it is one of the US's finest zoos. Opened in 1959 as a small-scale zoo and attraction, Busch Gardens has been transformed to the extent that it rivals Walt Disney World. Admission fees are high but include access to all exhibits and rides; parking is a few dollars more. There are many restaurants to choose from. Plan on devoting an entire day to the attractions, and be prepared to leave exhausted. Wear comfortable clothes and be prepared to get wet.

As on a real African safari, you can roam around the grounds and view the 3,000-plus animals, birds, and reptiles, representing more than 300 species. The park is divided into several theme regions. The **Serengeti Plain** is an 80-acre (32-ha) flatland where herds of antelope, giraffes, black rhinos and Asian elephants roam free. You can observe the animals from an elevated monorail or from a steam locomotive. **Stanleyville** is a recreation of an African village where you can take a ride on the **Tanganyika Tidal Wave**. The **Congo** exhibit, home to rare white Bengal tigers, offers a feisty white-water raft ride down the 'Congo River.' The **Morocco** exhibit features an exotic walled city, palace, snake charmers and Marrakesh theater. Other attractions include a roller-coaster, an elephant preserve, a koala habitat, an animal nursery, an exotic bird garden, ice-skating shows, and country-music extravaganzas.

Right: entertaining the visitors, and the residents, at Busch Gardens

9. ST PETERSBURG *(see map, p38)*

A full day in the St Petersburg area, with breakfast on the Municipal Pier, a trip to the Salvador Dalí Museum, and an afternoon on the beach.

The city of **St Petersburg**, which occupies a narrow peninsula west of Tampa Bay and east of the Gulf of Mexico, is both a retirement community and a vacation playground. It can be reached from Tampa by four causeways: all have signs that lead you to the downtown or beach areas. If you have only a day to spend in St Petersburg, prepare to make it a long one.

The downtown district is along the bayside of the city and most of its attractions are adjacent to the St Petersburg **Municipal Pier** (daily 10am–9pm). A long, runway-like road leads out to the pier's main building – a five-story, inverted pyramid structure with a panoramic view of Tampa Bay. For a few dollars you can park in a huge parking lot at the foot of the pier for the whole day; admission to the pier is free.

A Museum for Children

Originally a railroad pier built in 1889, the pier was rebuilt in 1973 and turned into a festive marketplace in 1988. It is full of gift shops, art galleries, a unique vertical aquarium, restaurants, and cafés. Musicians, mime artists, and jugglers entertain the crowds as seagulls and pelicans soar overhead. Attractions aside, the fresh muffins and cappuccino you can get on the pier justify an early-morning visit. If you have children to entertain, the

pier's **Great Explorations** (daily 10am–8pm) is always a good option. A hands-on museum, it has six exhibit areas that range in focus from health to science and the arts. It also has a rock-climbing wall, a touch tunnel, and a body shop where visitors can test their physical strength and flexibility. A welcome recent addition to the pier area is **Baywalk** (daily 10am–midnight), an ultra-modern, peach-colored entertainment complex that incorporates a 24-screen movie theater, and plenty of stores, restaurants, and bars.

The marina on the east side of the pier has hundreds of sailboats – some for rent – and the surrounding waters are a popular place for jet-ski races. On the north side of the entrance to the pier, on NE Second Avenue, is the **St Petersburg Historical Museum** (Tues–Sat 10am–5pm, Sun 1–5pm), which features changing exhibits on St Petersburg and Florida history. Across the street on Beach Drive the **Museum of Fine Arts** (Tues–Sat 10am–5pm, Sun 1–5pm) houses American, French Impressionist, Far Eastern, and pre-Columbian art.

About two blocks away from the art museum at 100 Second Street North is the **Florida International Museum** (daily 9am–7pm). Housed in a transformed department store, this museum is an affiliate of the Smithsonian Institution in Washington, DC. In addition to a permanent exhibit on US Pres-

Above: the Salvador Dalí Museum features some of the Spanish surrealist's finest works

BROOKLINE BOOKSMITH

Independent Store For Independent Minds
279 Harvard Street
Brookline, MA 02146
(617) 566-6660
www.brooklinebooksmith.com

505743 Reg 1 5:11 pm 12/24/01

S FLORIDA PKT	1 @ 13.95	13.95
S FLORIDA	1 @ 19.95	19.95
SUBTOTAL		33.90
SALES TAX - 5%		1.70
TOTAL		35.60
MASTER CARD PAYMENT		35.60

PUBLISHERS WEEKLY'S
BOOKSELLER OF THE YEAR 1998!!!!

CHECK OUT OUR 10% DISCOUNTS
BARGAIN BOOKS AT UP TO 80% OFF!!!

ident John F. Kennedy, the museum hosts collections, often with a slight political slant, from around the world. Past shows have included exhibits on the Cuban Missile Crisis, Treasures from the Russian czars, and the Incas of South America. Not far away, on Fifth Street South, is the **Florida Holocaust Memorial Museum** (Mon–Fri 10am–5pm, Sat, Sun noon–5pm). Founded by a Florida businessman who escaped Nazi Germany, it contains a few somber artifacts from the war, including a boxcar used to transport Jews to Auschwitz. But for the most part the museum focuses on tolerance education, Jewish religious life, and the history of anti-Semitism.

If you have enough time to visit only one museum, you might well choose the **Salvador Dalí Museum** (Tues–Sat 9.30am–5.30pm, Sun noon–5.30pm). To get there, drive east on Second Avenue from the pier and turn left again on Third Street. At the end of the street you will see the large white museum. One of the finest art centers in the country, the museum, opened in 1982, houses a permanent exhibit that you would expect to find in New York, Madrid, or Paris. The collection consists of some of the Spanish surrealist's finest and most famous works, including 93 oil paintings, 200 watercolors and drawings, and 1,000 prints. It is said to be the largest collection of his work in the world. Narrated tours of the museum, including a biography of Dalí, are offered at intervals throughout the day, and the gift shop sells signed lithographs, wall-posters, and some cleverly designed melting watches.

Art of the Shuffleboard

If you have time on your way to the beach, you might want to check out one of St Petersburg's claims to fame – serious shuffleboard competitions. The art of pushing clay disks with a long stick towards the highest scoring spot on the board is an art form in St Petersburg, as can be seen at the **National Shuffleboard Hall of Fame** (Mon–Fri 9am–1pm). To get there, retrace the drive back to the pier and head east on Second Avenue until Mirror Lake Drive. As part of the St Petersburg Shuffleboard Club – the nation's oldest and largest such club – the Hall of Fame is a hokey shrine to some of the city's finest shufflers. There is no admission fee and the club's director can often be prevailed upon to take you on a tour and explain the history of the sport.

Above: one of St Petersburg's many sandy beaches

If you are ready for lunch and a stroll, or swim, head for the **Gulf Beaches**. Several causeways take you westward from the downtown area to the long string of beaches that includes several seaside communities as well as St Pete Beach. Most of the beach towns have so far resisted the onslaught of high-rise hotels and condominiums that have enveloped most of the eastern Florida coast. Instead, the Suncoast beaches are packed with small, mom-and-pop motels, casual restaurants, and easy-going playgrounds.

From the northern to the southernmost tip of the beach strip, **Gulf Boulevard** passes through the towns of Clearwater, Indian Rocks Beach, Madeira Beach, Treasure Island and then finally **St Pete Beach**. For lunch, stop off at **Cracker's Bar and Grill** on Gulf Boulevard overlooking St Pete Beach. Some of the best choices on Cracker's menu that you might not find at home include fried alligator, grilled dolphin fish (not to be confused with the marine mammal), raw oysters and Creole jambalaya. For some post-prandial relax-

ation, this is a good spot for a beach walk. Aside from small parking fees, access to the beaches is free. The **St Pete Municipal Beach** is a broad affair with clumps of wild sea-oats, dressing-rooms, and snack bars. Volleyball, kite-flying, and para-sail rides from speedboats are popular. The area is also good for shelling.

Fitzgerald's Favorite

If you continue driving on Gulf Boulevard south of the Municipal Beach, you'll see the ornate, pink rococo palace that is the **Don CeSar Beach Resort** on your right. Built in the 1920s, the grand old hotel was once a favorite hideaway of author F Scott Fitzgerald; in its first incarnation it epitomized ostentatious living. But it fell into disrepair and by 1971 it was an eyesore. A restoration was finished in the 1980s, and the Don CeSar is once again the first-class, flamingo-pink beauty of its past. You don't have to be a hotel guest to wander around the pool or take a peek inside the hotel where antique shops, fancy boutiques, and art galleries dot the lobby.

A few miles south of the Don CeSar is **Fort De Soto Park** (open dawn to dusk), one of the most pristine and natural beaches on the central Gulf Coast. South of St Pete Beach, Fort De Soto can be reached by taking Gulf Boulevard east to the Pinellas Bayway and then driving south. Access to the park, and parking, is free, but a highway toll booth charges a small fee.

The 900-acre (364-ha) park, made up of six islands, is a historic site dating back to the Spanish-American War. You can wander around the old fort that once protected the coast from Spanish fleets, and watch the tankers make their way into Tampa Bay. As well as quiet, isolated beaches, the park has a fishing pier, picnic areas and a camp ground. Lush mangroves, dotted with water birds, surround the park grounds. In the summer porpoises often play in the waters near the shore, and swimmers can get close to them.

Above: the ornate, flamingo-pink rococo palace that is the Don CeSar Beach Resort
Right: the mall marina on Miami's Bayfront

Miami & the South

I f the popular images were anything to go by, Miami would be a city of drug-smuggling villains, designer-dressed cops, rainbow-colored skyscrapers, and old Art Deco hotels. As ever, the reality is more prosaic. Situated in Miami-Dade County and bordered by the Atlantic Ocean, Greater Miami contains about 28 different municipalities and has a population of about two million. More than half of its residents are foreign-born – sometimes the city feels more South American or Caribbean than American. The ability to speak a little Spanish frequently comes in handy here.

The downtown district attracts shoppers from as far afield as Caracas, Bogotá, Nassau, and Kingston. It is also where Miami's thriving international banking industry and the busy cruise and commercial port are to be found.

10. DOWNTOWN MIAMI *(see map, p46)*

A full day in downtown Miami, beginning with the boutiques and art galleries at Biscayne Bay. Afterward ride on the Metromover and walk down Flagler Street to the Metro-Dade Cultural Plaza.

Bayside Marketplace (daily 9am–midnight), located on the water at Biscayne Boulevard, is the best place from which to start a day tour of downtown Miami. Entrance to the marketplace is free; parking costs a few dollars. Bayside is a 16-acre (6-ha) shopping and entertainment complex of restaurants, bars, boutiques, kiosks, and art galleries. Lively from morning till night, Bayside can easily take about four hours to explore. Live music such as salsa, jazz, reggae, and pop floats through the air, and an array of boats – catamarans, gondolas, sailboats – is available for a quick sail around Biscayne Bay. Check out Art by God, a gallery specializing in animal bones, fossils, mounted fish, antlers, shark jaws, bearskin rugs, and primitive art. Although not the kind of place to appeal to animal-rights advocates, it is one of the more interesting stores to be found in the Miami area.

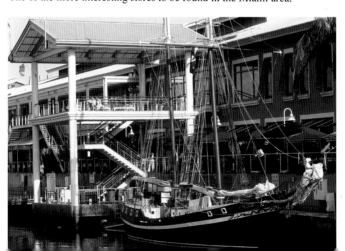

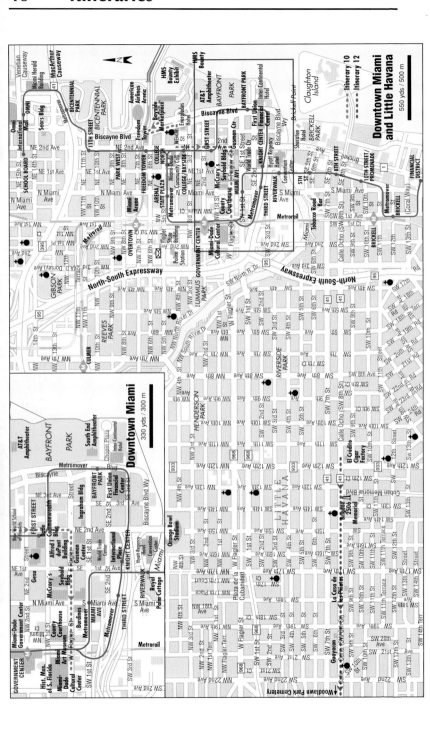

Exiting Bayside Marketplace you find yourself facing **Freedom Tower**, a peach-colored Mediterranean Revival building on Biscayne Boulevard. Built in 1925, the Freedom Tower was once the home of the now defunct *Miami News*, but acquired its name during the 1960s when it served as a processing center for Cuban refugees seeking freedom in Miami. To the south of Bayside Marketplace, also on Biscayne Boulevard, is **Bayfront Park**, a large, breeze-filled playground that often hosts outdoor concerts and ethnic festivals. At the eastern edge of the park is a statue of Christopher Columbus given to the city of Miami by the Italian government in 1953. At the southern end, a memorial designed by Isamu Noguchi honors the astronauts and crew who died when the space shuttle *Challenger* exploded in 1986.

A Bird's-Eye View of the City

For a quick orientation of downtown Miami, take a ride on the **Metromover**. Designed to make getting around downtown easy, the Metromover is popular with tourists who want a bird's-eye view of the city. Cross Biscayne Boulevard, walk west on NE Fourth Street about two blocks and you will find the College/Bayside Metromover Station on NE Second Ave. Deposit 25¢ in the turnstile, walk up the stairs and board the little green and white train. Both inner and outer loop rides describe a 10-minute jaunt through downtown, eventually returning to the station. Look out for the 47-story, three-tiered **NationsBank Tower**. Formerly the CenTrust Tower, the building looks spectacular at night when the series of colored lights on its facade are lit up. Sometimes it's pink, sometimes blue, and sometimes it is a kaleidoscope of colors.

After the short train tour, exit down the stairs and continue walking down NE Second Avenue. You will be facing the Wolfson Campus of Miami-Dade Community College, one of the largest community colleges in the US. Walk four blocks south until you come to East Flagler Street and turn right. Flagler Street, the main commercial artery, is full of electronics, jewelry, and clothing stores. Although congested and

Above: hoping for a gold rush
Right: the Metromover is a fun form of transportation

miami and the south

somewhat dilapidated, it is a good place for bargains. Also on Flagler is the **Gusman Center for the Performing Arts**, an ornate Spanish-style theater built in the 1920s. A little farther on Flagler is the **Alfred I duPont Building**, a classic Art Deco office building erected in the 1930s. And at 38 East Flagler Street is the **Flagler Station Mall** (Mon–Sat 10am–6pm), a shopping mall that hosts the **Floridita Restaurant**. Famous in Cuba before its owners migrated to Miami, the Floridita is good for pastries and coffee.

About a block past the Floridita look out for the **Dade County Courthouse**, a huge, neoclassical structure built in the 1920s. At the major intersection to the west of the courthouse, East Flagler becomes West Flagler Street, where you will find the **Miami-Dade Cultural Plaza**. Follow the ramp beside the flowing pools of water and you will find yourself in the plaza's main courtyard, a grand, Italian-style piazza that is popular at lunchtime with the downtown office crowd. There's also a refreshment stand on the plaza.

Exploring the three buildings around the plaza is a great way to avoid the heat of a downtown afternoon. The **Miami-Dade Public Library** (Mon–Thur 8am–9pm, Fri 8am–4.30pm, Sat 9am–1pm; free admission) contains a large collection of books and video cassettes, including a whole wing devoted to Miami and Florida.

Seminole Crafts

In the very center of the plaza, the **Historical Museum of Southern Florida** (Mon–Wed, Fri, Sat 10am–5pm, Thur 10am–9pm, Sun noon–5pm; small entrance fee) explains the history of South Florida from the days when Native Americans lived on the banks of the Miami River to the present. Its collection includes an old Miami trolley-car and lots of historic artifacts depicting the mass exodus of Cuban exiles to Miami. The museum gift shop sells a selection of Seminole Indian crafts and local art. The excellent **Miami Art Museum** (Tues–Fri 10am–5pm, Sat, Sun noon–5pm; small entrance fee) features classical and modern art.

Above: modern art at the excellent Miami Art Museum
Left: sculpture in the Miami-Dade Cultural Plaza

11. SOUTH MIAMI BEACH *(see map, p50)*

Breakfast at the News Café; tour of Miami's historic Art Deco District.

In the past 10 years, Miami Beach, specifically South Miami Beach, has become America's Riviera and a trendy resort for celebrities. At the southern tip of the barrier island that is Miami Beach, South Beach is a dense neighborhood of whimsical architecture, casual outdoor cafés and a bustling street life. It's a delightful place for a walking tour and can easily be reached from Miami proper by way of the MacArthur Causeway. As you drive east along the causeway you will see the behemoth cruise ships that line the docks of the port of Miami, the largest cruise port in the world.

At its end the causeway becomes Fifth Street and you will pass the Miami Beach marina on your right. Continue driving east until you reach Ocean Drive and turn left. This is the beginning of the historic Art Deco District that runs from Sixth to 23rd streets along the ocean, and west to Alton Road. The district has the largest collection of Art Deco architecture in the world, including more than 500 Deco buildings, some perfectly preserved, others in dilapidated shape. In recent years the district has become a popular location for fashion shoots so be prepared to find dozens of long-legged models lounging around in front of the quirky pastel-colored buildings.

SoBe It

A good spot to start a tour of South Beach (known as SoBe to locals) is at the **News Café** (daily 24-hours) on Ocean Drive and Eighth Street. The News is a European-style café, newsstand and jazz club combined. One of the hottest places on the beach, it is always busy and getting a table can take a while. But the food is terrific and the people-watching even better. After refreshment at the News, begin the colorful stroll up Ocean Drive.

A block away is the Waldorf Towers, a yellow, purple, and white Art Deco gem. Across the street is Volleyball Beach, where young and beautiful beach bums hang out. On the same street you'll find the Café des Arts, an elegant pink apartment building with a fine French restaurant on the first floor. At 10th Street is the Miami Beach Ocean Front Auditorium, a place where local people congregate for lectures, lunches and music.

A few blocks to the north at 10th Street and Ocean Drive is the **Art Deco Welcome Center** (daily 11am–9pm or later), run by the Miami Design Preservation League, which is responsible for the preservation of Miami Beach's Art Deco architecture. The center sells Art Deco antiques and jewelry, books, and postcards, and is a good place to learn about the history of Art Deco. Saturday morning walking tours of the district depart from the gift shop.

Right: the fresh face of Art Deco

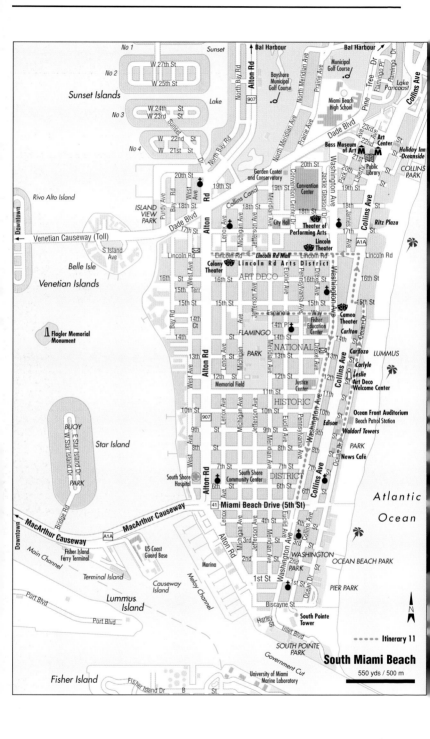

South Miami Beach

Itinerary 11

N

550 yds / 500 m

The next block features three more classic Art Deco hotels – the Carlyle, Cardozo, and Cavalier – that were among the first of the beach hotels to be restored. They are all spectacular structures and well-run hotels. To the east of Ocean Drive is Lummus Park, eight blocks of wide, white beachfront where kite-flyers, sunbathers, and joggers all jockey for space. At the northern end of Ocean Drive, just past the blue and white Betsy Ross Hotel, turn left at 15th Street, walk one block and you will be on **Collins Avenue**, the address of grand 1950s hotels such as the Eden Roc and the Fontainebleau.

Walk one block north on Collins Avenue and you will reach the Lincoln Road Mall. At the corner of Lincoln Road and Collins is the world's only Art Deco Burger King. It is housed in one of South Beach's classic pink and green Deco structures. Turn left and walk down Lincoln Road, a pedestrian-only street that was once one of Miami Beach's most upscale shopping districts. In the past few years Lincoln Road has been part of the South Beach renaissance and many of the old shops have been turned into art galleries and fine restaurants. Although there are still a few junky little stores lining the street, Lincoln Road has been entirely remodeled. It is home to the South Florida Art Center, a collective of over 100 local artists, the Lincoln Theater, home-base for Miami's New World Symphony, the Area Theater, a cozy and intimate playhouse, and the Miami City Ballet. At No 905 Lincoln Road, the ballet headquarters has a large window where locals come to watch the dancers warm up and practice their steps.

Desi Arnaz's American Debut

Two other streets worth exploring in South Beach are **Washington Avenue** and **Espanola Way**. Washington is one block west and parallel to Collins Avenue. It's a busy street full of delicatessens, secondhand stores, restaurants, fruit markets, and bakeries. Espanola Way, one block west of Washington Avenue just south of 15th Street, is one of the prettiest streets on the beach. At the corner is the Miami Beach International Youth Hostel, also known as the Clay Hotel. The striking pink Mediterranean Revival building is where Cuban band leader Desi Arnaz made his American debut. Today the

Above: volleyball is part of the beach culture

building, which houses a hostel that is popular with young, European tourists, extends down the street and in places is adorned with hand-painted tiles and balconies. It served as the backdrop for TV's *Miami Vice*. If you want to do some serious shopping, Espanola Way also has a unique collection of vintage clothing outlets, antique jewelry stores, and art boutiques.

12. LITTLE HAVANA *(see map, p46)*

Miami's Little Havana neighborhood offers the most intense Cuban experience on the American side of the Gulf Stream. Little Havana makes for a lively afternoon's excursion that will introduce you to a culture that is full of warmth, bravado, and a zest for life.

Located to the west of downtown, the heart of Little Havana – known in the neighborhood as **Calle Ocho** – lies along SW Eighth Street. A stroll down Calle Ocho will be enlivened by ethnic encounters, bursts of salsa music from the stores and houses, and the smell of garlic wafting through the air. Calle Ocho is the site of the annual, 23-block Cuban street festival – also, somewhat confusingly, known as Calle Ocho – in March.

Starting at the eastern part of the street not far from 11th Avenue, you will come across the **El Credito Cigar Factory** (Mon–Sat 8am–5pm). Founded in Cuba in 1907, El Credito is a working cigar factory seems to be in something of a time warp – you might think that you are in Havana *circa* 1950. The workers spend all day chopping tobacco and hand-rolling the potent-smelling cigars that for a long time were Cuba's most famous product. Few of the staff speak English, but visitors are welcome for a quick tour.

House of Tricks

Nearby is the **Botanica la Abuela** (Mon–Sat 10am–5pm), a Cuban-style pharmacy that sells paraphernalia for the Afro-Cuban religion of Santeria. Not far from 13th Avenue and Eighth Street you will find **La Casa de Los Trucos** (House of Tricks; Mon–Sat 10am–6pm), another Havana transplant and neighborhood institution that specializes in magic tricks, masks, cos-

tumes, and silly toys for adults and children alike.

Across the street is **Los Pinarenos** (Mon–Sat 9am–5pm), an open-air Cuban market that is especially good for tropical fruits and fresh vegetables. At the western corner of 13th Avenue (also known as Cuban Memorial Boulevard) and Eighth Street is the **Brigade 2506 Memorial**, a somber monument that pays tribute to the Cuban men who lost their lives in President Kennedy's failed 'Bay of Pigs' invasion of Cuba in 1961. Schoolchildren often come to the monument to place flowers and say a prayer alongside the flame.

At the corner of Eighth Street and 15th Avenue is **Maximo Gomez Park** or, as it is more commonly known, Domino Park. Elderly Cuban expatriates gather in this small, fenced-in park for games of dominos. The Spanish-speaking, cigar-smoking gentlemen talk about the good old days in their native Cuba, and dream about the day when they can return to their beloved country. By a strange convention, the park custom is supposed to be for the exclusive use of men over the age of 55, but in reality all visitors are welcome.

Farther west on Eighth Street, near 21st Avenue, is **Bellas Artes** (tel: 305-325 0515), a Spanish-language theater that specializes in Latin productions. The plays, which range from classic dramas to contemporary comedies about hard times in Castro's Cuba, usually form a great spectacle, with the audience often the source of as much fun as the actual performance.

Somosa's Grave

Toward the western end of Little Havana's Calle Ocho, at 32nd Avenue, is the **Woodlawn Park Cemetery** (daily 10am–5pm). The cemetery's peaceful, tree-lined grounds are dotted with elaborate and well-maintained tombs. Nmerous well-known Cubans – including three former presidents of the island – are buried here. Also laid to rest here is Anastasio Somosa, whose notorious dictatorship of Nicaragua lasted from 1963 until his overthrow in 1979. Somosa's family operates several restaurants in Miami.

For a final stop in the Eighth Street area, you can't do better than to sample a home-style Cuban dinner at the **Versailles Restaurant** (daily 8am–2am) on 35th Avenue. A long-established favorite among the local Cuban community, Versailles is a noisy and garish spot that has become a celebrated neighborhood landmark. The meals are reasonably priced and typical of the robust cooking for which Cuban grandmothers are famous. Recommended are the roast pork, fried bananas, and *arroz con pollo* (rice with chicken).

Left: Maximo Gomez Park is commonly known as Domino Park
Above: Little Havana is full of friendly faces and convenient stores

13. COCONUT GROVE *(see map, p55)*

A day tour of the stores and tropical architecture that give Miami's vibrant Coconut Grove neighborhood a sophisticated, cosmoplitan air.

Located a few miles south of downtown and east of US1, the center of Coconut Grove is best reached by driving east from US1 at the intersection of McDonald Street until you reach Grand Avenue. Public parking areas are scattered throughout the center district; most require coins for the meters.

One of the oldest and lushest areas of Miami, Coconut Grove is a colorful neighborhood of funky houses with a spirited center of outdoor cafés, shops and galleries that hums with street life day and night. Once a mecca for artists and writers, the Grove has in recent years, leaned more toward commercial enterprises, but it still attracts countless Miamians at weekends.

To the south of McDonald Street on Grand Avenue you will find the Bahamian neighborhood of the Grove. In the late 19th century, many of the Bahamas' residents settled in the area to help build the city. Their presence is still prominent and the neighborhood is full of small, island-style houses.

From McDonald Street eastward to Mary Street, Grand Avenue is full

of commercial activity. Near Virginia Street and Grand Avenue is the shopping and entertainment center of **CocoWalk** (Sun–Thur 11am–10pm; Fri, Sat 11am–midnight). This multi-level pink and white complex is full of chain stores, boutiques, bars, and restaurants, and has an eight-screen movie theater. The center courtyard, adorned with towering palm trees, often has live music at night and on weekends. Some of the more lively bars are on the upper levels: Tu Tu Tango, Baja Beach Club, and Hooters are all boisterous places that attract a young crowd. Also upstairs is the Improv Comedy Club, a sophisticated dinner club that rarely fails to amuse.

Upscale Shopping

Across the street from CocoWalk is **Mayfair in the Grove**, another shopping and restaurant complex with the plush 180-room Mayfair House hotel as the centerpiece. More sophisticated than CocoWalk, the Mayfair has more exclusive stores. Although not the place to pick up a bargain, it is worth looking around. One of its more offbeat outlets is the Oak Feed Store (daily 10am–9pm), a well-stocked health foods store and restaurant. It is also home to **Planet Hollywood**, the movie memorabilia theme-restaurant chain.

Back toward the west end of Grand Avenue is **Commodore Plaza**, a fashionable, one-block street jam-packed with cafés and stores. On the south side of Commodore is the Grove Harbour Courtyard, a three-level complex of shops and restaurants. Also in the complex is the Carlos Art Gallery (Mon–Sat

Above: one aspect of the shopping and entertainment center that is CocoWalk
Above Left: cruising the streets in a convertible is a favorite activity with the young

11am–9pm, Sun 11am–6pm), one of the best Haitian art galleries in the city. Next door on the second-floor is the Kaleidoscope, an elegant tropical restaurant with a first-class menu. The end of Commodore Plaza intersects with Main Highway, another busy street in the Grove. Both corners of the intersection are filled by outdoor cafés that make excellent spots for people-watching.

A few blocks to the south on Main Highway is the Coconut Grove Playhouse, an intimate little theater built in 1926. Next door is the **Taurus**, a popular steak-house that attracts a happy-hour crowd of professionals on weeknights. Across the street from here, tucked away behind old banyan trees, is the **Barnacle State Historic Site** (Thur–Sun 9am–4pm). The former home of Miami pioneer Ralph Munroe, the Barnacle is a perfectly preserved 100-year-old house furnished with period antiques, lace curtains, and oriental rugs. Designed with a natural air-conditioning system of vents and fans, it catches the breezes that blow off Biscayne Bay, and is a fine example of what life in Miami was like in its early days. The small entrance fee is well worth the price and includes a narrated tour of the house and grounds.

The south side of Main Highway is lined with ice-cream parlors, clothing and swimwear boutiques, and gift shops. It ends at the intersection with McFarlane Road, which slopes down a hill toward **Peacock Park**, a waterfront playground that hosts festivals and concerts throughout the year. At the foot of McFarlane Road is South Bayshore Drive, a road that leads past the **Dinner Key Marina** where hundreds of yachts are moored.

miami and the south

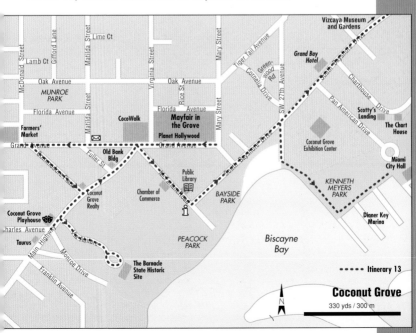

Coconut Grove

330 yds / 300 m

• • • • Itinerary 13

Continue on South Bayshore Drive and, a few miles to the north, you will reach the **Vizcaya Museum and Gardens** (daily 9.30am–5pm; gardens till 5.30pm). Built around 1915, Vizcaya is a 70-room Italian Renaissance-style palace. More than 10,000 laborers were employed for a construction that includes Cuban barrel tile roofs and wrought-iron grillwork. The former winter home of the American industrialist James Deering, Vizcaya is full of European antiques, art, and tapestries, and attracts over 250,000 visitors a year.

The 10-acre (4-ha) grounds are manicured European-style gardens with decorative urns, statues, and fountains and a series of islands connected by bridges. An outdoor café, nestled beside a coral rock grotto and swimming-pool, serves surprisingly good food and drinks. On Brickell Avenue, just to the north, is a Madonna's bayfront mansion. Paparazzi often hide in the bushes in the hope of catching 'the Material Girl' frolicking in the sun.

14. THE EVERGLADES *(see map, p56)*

A morning excursion to the Everglades National Park.

Bring a hat, sun-block lotion, and, in summer, mosquito repellent. Do not feed the alligators. They are wild creatures and have been known to bite off arms.

Although the charms of **Everglades National Park** can be quite subtle – ripples on the water as an alligator passes, a mild flutter when an egret takes its leave from the branches of a tree, or a slight change in the color of the grass as the breeze blows through the air – the park has a reputation for fascinating travelers from around the world with its vast wetlands. Located about 25 miles (40km) west of Miami on the **Tamiami Trail** (Eighth Street), the Everglades make for a peaceful morning excursion from the city. Given that the afternoons are awfully hot, and that much of the park's wildlife activity takes place early in the morning, it's best to plan on reaching the park by 8am.

Once you have driven past the ugly shopping centers and suburban housing complexes, the first hint that you are in Native American territory is supplied by the **Miccosukee Resort and Convention Center** on SW 177th Avenue. Recently built, this glaringly ultra-modern complex is both a luxury hotel and high-stakes gambling casino that features live entertainment along with a bingo hall, poker tables, video slot machines, and a glittering teen arcade. Although traditional Miccosukee culture teaches that gambling is immoral, tribal members have created a lucrative niche in this business, and profits do indeed tickle down to all members of the tribe. Continuing west a few miles past the Miccosukee Resort, the Tamiami Trail becomes a quiet two-lane highway surrounded by the fresh waters of the Everglades.

A Reslient Ecosystem

A shallow, slow-moving river that looks like a field of wet grass, the Everglades – which is about 100 miles (160km) long by 50 miles (80km) wide – provides south Florida with most of its water. Because of this it is at the center of one Florida's most controversial environmental struggles. Severely damaged by Hurricane Andrew in 1992, the Everglades' ecosystem is resilient; ecologists say that the physical damage suffered by plant and animal life was nature's way of cleaning out the old in preparation for the new. Regular Everglades visitors can still point out the places that were badly damaged, but now new growth has taken hold and first-time visitors can barely notice a trace.

It's not possible to visit all the spots on the Tamiami Trail in one morning or even in a whole day, so you should choose between:

- taking a thrilling airboat ride
- walking amidst the wilds of nature
- mingling with Native Americans.

Coopertown's (daily 8am–7pm) is one of several outfits that offers airboat rides in the Everglades. Of the choice available, Coopertown's is perhaps the least commercial and most fun. For a reasonable price, a guide takes you out in a flat-bottom boat for an exciting, noisy 30-minute ride.

Just west of Coopertown's is **Everglades Safari Park** (daily

Above Left: the Italian Renaissance-style Vizcaya Museum palace
Right: the pelican is one of a huge variety of Floridian birds

8.30am–5pm). Very popular with the tour-bus crowd, the safari park is a rustic complex with quiet nature trails, boat rides, a wildlife museum, and craft shop. Further along the trail is the entrance to **Shark Valley** (daily 8.30am–6pm; entrance fee). Part of Everglades National Park, Shark Valley is run by the National Parks Service and is one of the least commercial stops on the trail. Located at the headwaters of the Shark River, it is a secluded spot with a helpful information center. A heavy, musky smell from its dense plant life hangs in the air. A 15-mile road loops through the park and can be explored by taking one of the narrated tram tours, renting a bicycle, or by walking. An observation tower inside the grounds offers a broad view of the surrounding wetlands, and affords visitors an overview of manatees stirring in the waters, water birds feeding in the marsh, tree frogs perched in palms, wild orchids, bald eagles, otters, pelicans, flamingos, spoonbills, alligators and turtles sunning on the banks, and people paddling in canoes. Although they are both endangered species, Florida panthers and American crocodiles inhabit the Shark Valley park, though they are rarely seen even from the observation tower.

A Native American Reservation

About one mile (2km) past Shark Valley is the **Miccosukee Indian Village and Restaurant** (daily 9am–5pm; entrance fee). A Native American reservation, the Miccosukee Village has more than 500 residents, and dozens of authentic palm-thatch huts. Once part of the Creek Nation (an association of clan villages in Georgia and Alabama), the Miccosukee tribe now has domestic nation status, and operates as a sovereign territory and distinct political entity. It has had its own constitution and bylaws since the 1960s, and today is a fairly self-sufficient community with its own tribal government, police department, court system, medical clinic, day-care center, school, senior citizens center, and numerous other social welfare programs. Although the tribe gets most of its revenues from the casino and other

Above: exploring the Everglades on foot
Left: an Everglades native

commercial endeavors, many of its members use traditional methods of hunting, fishing, and farming in the surrounding lands.

For the tourist, a visit offers the opportunity to learn more about the tribe through village tours. These include lessons on their language (Mikasuki), lifestyle, religion, cooking, natural medicines, woodcarving, basket weaving, beadwork, sewing, and doll making. There are alligator wrestling demonstrations, a nature trail, a museum filled with historical artifacts, and a gift shop that sells moccasins, hats, jewelry, silver pottery, paintings, historic photographs, stuffed alligator heads, and the Miccosukee's unique patchwork fabric clothing made from tiny squares of brightly colored cloth.

Even if you don't want to take a full tour of the reservation, the Miccosukee Restaurant is the trail's best lunch option. It has an airy view of the water, and serves traditional Native American foods such as pumpkin and Indian fried bread, fried catfish, frogs' legs, and gatortail. After a hot, sweaty morning, you might want to wash such ethnic cuisine down with an ice-cold beer.

15. FORT LAUDERDALE *(see map, p61)*

A full day's exploration of both the traditional old structures and the exciting new innovations of downtown Fort Lauderdale, taking in assorted museums, historic homes, and waterfront entertainment.

An easy 45-minute drive north of Miami via I-95, Fort Lauderdale has a totally different personality from its big sister to the south. It has a very 'American' character, and little of the multi-ethnic atmosphere that permeates Miami. It is an exceptionally clean, pretty, and laid-back city, with a network of approximately 300 miles (480 km) of navigable canals and waterways.

The town is most noted for its seven miles (11km) of broad beaches and its wealthy yachting community. Most of its popular attractions are located on the waterfront.

About 25 years ago Fort Lauderdale was notorious for its annual spring-break bacchanalia that attracted hundreds of thousands of college students from across the US. But by the early 1990s, local residents finally grew weary and city officials began to restrict the students' activities. Soon after their numbers dwindled, and spring break is now a shadow of what it once was. As a part of the city's clean-up plans, it poured millions of dollars into the redevelopment of The Strip, a central beachfront area that once housed seedy, honky-tonk bars.

Affluent Enclave

Now successfully reincarnated, Fort Lauderdale caters to affluent tourists who come to take in the sun, play along

Right: Fort Lauderdale pleasure boats

the waterways, dine in fine restaurants, and shop at its many art galleries and upscale stores. It has a concentrated downtown district that is both easy and fun to explore. Although the downtown business district is characterised by towering chrome-and-glass skyscrapers, the nearby historic district is a laid-back neighborhood with old-fashioned gaslights, small museums, and extraordinary boutiques.

For a quick nautical jaunt through the city, entertaining tours can easily be arranged through **Water Taxi of Fort Lauderdale** (daily 10am–midnight; tel: 954-467 6677). As well as offering a regularly scheduled route down the New River, with designated stops at several of the area's attractions, these comfortable old vessels can also be hired for personalized day tours and will shuttle passengers anywhere they want to go. They are also available in the evenings, when they provide a safe, convenient, and novel night on the town that includes stops at some of Fort Lauderdale's most popular watering holes.

Tickets for the water taxi are relatively inexpensive and may be purchased for one way, round-trip, or all-day cruising.

Florida's Most Popular Museum

For a walking tour of the area, the **Museum of Discovery and Science** (Mon–Sat 10am–5pm, Sun noon–6pm) on SW Second Street is a good place to start. The largest science museum in south Florida, this interactive museum was designed with children in mind, and includes an IMAX 3D movie theater, hands-on science exhibits, video games, a simulated journey to the moon, bubble-making experiments, rats that play basketball, and a kinetic energy sculpture called the Great Gravity Clock. Although the museum caters primarily to young people, adults also seem to love it. It is therefore hardly surprising that it is the most-visited museum in the state.

A few blocks away at No 219 SW Second Avenue is the **Fort Lauderdale Historical Museum** (Tues–Sat 10am–5pm). Built in 1905, this structure, formerly the New River Inn, explains the birth and growth of the city up until the 1940s. Alongside the exhibits, it runs constant screening of silent movies made in Fort Lauderdale during the 1920s.

Not far away on SW First Avenue is **Las Olas Riverfront** (Sun–Thur 10am–11pm, Fri, Sat 11am–midnight), a much more modern addition to the neighborhood. A sprawling, open-air entertainment center, the Riverfront was designed with Disney in mind and has an atmosphere of a well-tended, all-American small town. Complete with Spanish tile roofs, waterfront gazebos, an inner courtyard, and pushcart vendors, it's a festive, high-energy complex filled with bars, restaurants, and shops. It also features a virtual

Above: the Great Gravity Clock at the Museum of Discovery and Science
Right: on the waterfront – waterways and canals abound in Fort Lauderdale

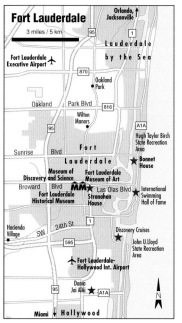

miami and the south

rollercoaster ride, a video arcade, bumper cars, movie theaters, and round-the-clock live music.

Arcane Specialty Shops

Around the corner from the Riverfront is **Himmarshee Village**, also known as Olde Town. Named for the Native American word that means New Water, Himmarshee is a quaint and historic neighborhood full of architecture that is redolent of New Orleans. Many of the buildings have been renovated and transformed into a trendy cluster of arcane specialty shops and friendly neighborhood pubs. More authentic and less commercial than Las Olas Riverfront, Himmarshee Village features a number of independent breweries, plus cigar bars, jazz and blues clubs, as well as several small but interesting ethnic restaurants.

Just a few steps away from Himmarshee Village you will find **Riverwalk**, a peaceful, palm-lined waterfront promenade that meanders past a series of parks for several blocks along the north bank of the New River. Riverwalk eventually connects with **Las Olas Boulevard**, a broad, picturesque boulevard, much of whose romantic atmosphere is supplied by horse-drawn carriages that are available for rides.

At No 1 East Las Olas Boulevard is the **Fort Lauderdale Museum of Art** (Tues–Sat 10am–5pm, Sun noon–5pm). This impressive museum houses a collection of CoBrA art, a term used to describe a group of Expressionist painters from the European cities of Copenhagen, Brussels, and Amsterdam

who were known for their dramatic imagery and experimental works.

Another museum worth visiting, about five blocks east of the Fort Lauderdale Museum of Art, at Sixth Avenue and Las Olas Boulevard, is **Stranahan House** (Wed–Sat 10am–4pm, Sun 1–4pm). The oldest private home in the city, Stranahan House was built by local pioneer Frank Stranahan in 1901. For decades it served the nascent community as a town hall, post office, and trading post for Seminole Indians who, arriving on dugout canoes, brought their animal skins and alligator hides to sell at the house. These days the house is a museum that overlooks the New River. It is dedicated to south Florida's frontier days, and is filled with historic photographs, documents, and period antiques.

A Quirky Residence

One last spot worth checking out near the downtown area is **Bonnet House** (Wed–Fri 10am–1.30pm, Sat, Sun noon–3pm). Located on North Birch Road about a mile (2km) north of Las Olas Boulevard, Bonnet House is a plantation home constructed in 1921 for internationally acclaimed artist Frederick Clay Bartlett and his wife Evelyn. A verdant enclave comprising 35-acres (14-ha) in the middle of a highly developed stretch of beach, the property is still dotted with mango, avocado, orange, mulberry, guava, cherry, and calabash trees, and has dozens of resident squirrel monkeys, peacocks, swans, and parrots.

Named after the bonnet water lilies that once grew on the property, the grand old two-story house is now a veritable treasure trove of a museum with a carnival-like atmosphere that showcases the idiosyncratic lifestyle of the people who once lived here. Among the quirky finds from around the world on display are European antiques, African masks, Indonesian wood carvings, mounted game fish, massive turtle shells, porcelain dolls, Native American artifacts, Caribbean folk art, tapestries and textiles, jade and lapis carvings, and assorted whimsical carousel animals.

The Florida Keys

A chain of thousands of tropical islands (31 of them linked by road) that dangles off the southern tip of the Florida coast, the Florida Keys are divided into the Upper Keys, the Middle Keys, and, incorporating Key West, the Lower Keys. About 800 uninhabited islands surround them. To the south and east lies the Atlantic Ocean; to the west the Gulf of Mexico. Waiting temptingly at the end, about 35 miles (56km) south of Marathon and 155 miles (248km) south of Miami is Key West, the last of the islands.

Key West is a singular city – decadent, hedonistic, and a refuge for non-conformists. Its architecture combines New England and Caribbean styles, with pastel-colored gingerbread verandas, widow's walks, and wrought-iron balconies. The population of this small (4 miles/7km by 1½ miles/2.4 km) island is only 25,000, but over a million tourists visit annually.

Lots of visitors fly to Key West from Miami airport, and there is a Greyhound bus service that makes eight stops between Miami and Key West. The easiest way to reach the Keys, however, is to rent a car and hit the road.

16. THE FLORIDA KEYS *(see map, p56)*

A long, leisurely road trip south from Miami through the incomparable Florida Keys with stops in Key Largo, Islamorada, and Marathon.

Connected by a series of bridges, the only road that runs through the entire chain of Keys islands is **Overseas Highway**. From Miami you can choose between two routes: the Florida Turnpike, which winds up in Homestead, or I-95, which ends at the southern end of Miami, where it becomes US1. Both roads lead to Overseas Highway, where small green Mile Marker signs are posted at regular intervals. Just to the south of Florida City for example, the MM126 sign indicates that you are exactly 126 miles (200km) from Key West. As you travel south past ever-decreasing MM numbers, salt water permeates the air. The surrounding natural beauty – endless vistas and clear blue-green water on either side – is fabulous. From Miami, Key Largo is about an hour and a half away.

Just north of Key Largo at MM 102.5 is **John Pennekamp Coral Reef State Park** (daily 8am–sunset). The most visited state

Left: relaxation, Florida-style
Right: Islamorada is known for its big fish

park in Florida, and rigorously protected by federal laws, Pennekamp is one of the world's most popular diving spots. The park's coral reef, 3 miles (5km) offshore, is an eco-paradise filled with over 400 species of marine life, such as: starfish, lobsters, sharks, sponges, sea cucumbers, stingrays, barracuda, crabs, and angel fish. Scuba and snorkeling trips can be arranged from the information center; glass-bottom boat trips leave three times a day for two-hour tours of the reef. The most popular attraction in the park is **Key Largo Dry Rocks**, site of the bronze **Christ of the Deep** statue, a replica of the Christ of the Abyss in the Mediterranean, off Genoa, Italy.

Key Largo

Back on Overseas Highway at MM 106, the **Key Largo Chamber of Commerce** (daily 9am–5pm) offers free information to tourists. Key Largo was originally called Rock Harbor, until the popularity of the 1948 Humphrey Bogart movie *Key Largo* presaged a change of name. Parts of the film were shot at the **Caribbean Club**, a 24-hour-a-day saloon at MM 104, which features memorabilia about the movie. Another evocative place for Bogart fans is the **Holiday Inn Key Largo Resort**, where the original steam-powered boat from *The African Queen* is moored with a dummy of Bogart at the wheel. The boat can be hired by tourists for rides through local waters.

At MM102 is the **Maritime Museum** (daily 10am–5pm), whose exhibits record a history in which hundreds of ships have been wrecked along the Keys' reefs. Artifacts spanning 400 years include a reconstructed shipwreck, antique charts, cannons, gold bars, and items salvaged from *Henrietta Marie*,

Above: Christ of the Deep, off Key Largo
Left: Key Largo connection to Key West

a British slave ship that sank in 1700. Continuing south, pass through **Tavernier**, a sleepy little town founded in the late 19th century and most noted as the place where several 'Big Foot' sightings occurred in the 1970s. Local fishermen and residents claimed to spot the mythical, part-man part-beast roaming the mangrove swamps.

After crossing over Tavernier Creek, the next cluster of islands includes Plantation and **Windley Key**. At MM84.5 on Windley Key, the **Theater of the Sea** (daily 9.30am–5.45pm), the world's second-oldest marine park, has been entertaining tourists since 1946. Housed in the pits of an old railroad quarry, the 14-acre (6-ha) park has a 300-gallon 'living reef' aquarium, touch tank, alligator pond, shark pool, and about a dozen resident dolphins that put on an action-packed show. It also offers popular swim-with-the-dolphins encounters. About a mile (2km) to the south you will find the **Hurricane Memorial**, an Art Deco landmark that commemorates the 1935 hurricane that devastated the area, killing more than 400 people.

Fishing Capital of the World

Next stop is the town of **Islamorada** (pronounced *eye-lah-mor-ah-da*). Over the years Islamorada has been a major center for shipbuilding, sponge-diving, wreck-salvaging, and turtle farming, but these days it is known as the Fishing Capital of the World. Due to their proximity to the Gulf Stream, the offshore waters teem with big game fish, and the town hosts major tour-naments throughout the year. Dozens of charter-boat operators, marinas, and bait-and-tackle shops line Overseas Highway here. Local fishing guides can be hired, and several local restaurants will clean and cook your catch.

To get an idea of the importance of fishing to the local economy, it is worth stopping at the **Fishing Museum** (Mon–Sat 10am–5pm), inside Bud 'n' Mary's Marina at MM80. Although modest, this little museum has an inter-esting collection of antique fishing tackle, photos of big catches, and a library with information on the history of fishing in the Keys.

Islamorada is also well known for its hard-drinking bars, especially at the **Holiday Isle Resort**, a sprawling hotel containing 12 bars that are always packed out with people and pulsating with live music.

Continuing south for about 25 miles (40km), past **Long**, **Conch**, and **Grassy Keys**, at MM53 is **Marathon**, and the beginning of the Middle Keys. With a permanent population of about 14,000, Marathon is one of the largest communities in the island chain. Far more developed and congested than the towns in the Upper Keys, Marathon is also a big fishing destination. At MM50 is the **Crane Point Hammock** and **Museum of the Florida Keys**.

Right: nosy seals at the Theater of the Sea

A 63-acre (25-ha) nature sanctuary, Crane Point has North America's last virgin palm hammock. Inside the hammock is a substantial museum filled with exhibits on Keys history, botany, geology, and wildlife.

The southern end of Marathon leads to the **7-Mile Bridge**, the world's longest segmental bridge. Beyond the bridge is the **Bahia Honda State Recreation Area** (daily 8am–sunset). This 275-acre (112-ha) park backing on to the Atlantic Ocean, Bahia Honda has lush tropical trees and flowers, a deepwater lagoon, and includes one of Florida's best beaches.

17. KEY WEST *(see map, p67)*

A day's exploration of the Old Town and its maritime, literary, ethnic, and practical heritage. Adjourn to Sloppy Joe's for lunch. Choose from a number of wonderful museums and round off the day with a viewing of the sunset and an evening of live entertainment on Mallory Square.

Key West, the southernmost city in the continental US, is best explored by bicycle or on foot. The best place to begin a day's walking tour is on the waterfront on the western edge of Old Town. The area known as **Old Town**, in the western part of the island, is the focal point of most of Key West's colorful architecture and diverse attractions. Two parallel streets in particular – Whitehead and Duval – lend themselves to leisurely walking tours. Depending upon the number of stops you make, a stroll down one and then back up the other can take five to six hours, leaving you plenty of time to make it to Mallory Square to join the daily sunset celebrations.

The Conch Republic

The bicycle is the islanders' favored mode of transportation. Born-on-the-island locals call themselves conchs (pronounced *konks*), and 'conch cruisers' are their fat-tired bicycles. Such terminology reflects the locals' highly developed sense of identity: a few years ago the people of Key West declared themselves citizens of the Conch Republic, an island nation that wanted to secede from the USA.

For visitors one of the easiest ways to get acquainted with the city before venturing out on your own is to take a 90-minute **Conch Train** tour (frequent departures daily 9am–4.30pm from either Mallory Square or Roosevelt Avenue). Originally opened in 1958, the Conch Train features a series of open-air wagons pulled by an imitation locomotive that rattles through the city while the conductor points out spots of interest and explains the island's history and culture. The conductor, perhaps better described as a guide, will doubtless relate how, in the 19th century, Key West was a place full of sponge divers, cigar makers, and pirates. It was also the richest per capita city in the country. In recent years the island has enjoyed something of a renais-

Above: nautical twist
Above Right: treasure in the Mel Fisher Maritime Heritage Society Museum

sance, with dilapidated buildings being turned into restaurants, guesthouses, and art galleries. The gay contribution has been immense and the local calendar now features Fantasy Fest, a flamboyant costume-party street festival that is part gay pride parade, part Halloween bash. And the city still

has a considerable number of writers who call it home, although the days when the likes of Ernest Hemingway and Tennessee Williams were a part of the landscape are long gone.

Treasure Worth $4 Billion

On Greene Street, about two blocks from Whitehead Street, is the **Mel Fisher Maritime Heritage Society Museum** (daily 9.30am–5.30pm). Mel Fisher was a marine salvager who spent decades searching for sunken treasures

in the waters off Key West. In 1985 he amazed the world by finding a bounty of gold and silver bars, chains, coins, and jewels from two Spanish galleons – the *Atocha* and the *Santa Margarita* – that sank in 1622. The haul was valued at about $4 billion. Fisher, who was known for his bright red suspenders and the huge gold medallion he wore round his neck, would sit in the office at the rear of the museum, frequently emerging to meet visitors. The museum's nominal entrance fee entitles you to view the artifacts from the actual galleons, including a beautiful 77-carat emerald, while learning about the marine salvage industry. Fisher died in 1998.

The **Little White House Museum** (daily 9am–5pm) on the waterfront at the end of Greene Street, near the intersection of Whitehead Street, was built

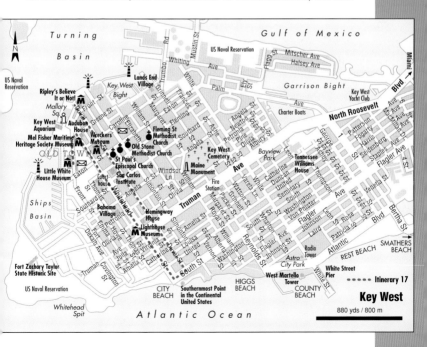

Key West
880 yds / 800 m

in 1890. Part of the **Truman Annex** complex, the Little White House was the winter vacation home of Harry S Truman. While president in the 1940s, Truman came here to swim, drink bourbon, and play poker. The museum offers a guided house tour and a movie chronicling the Truman era.

One block from Greene Street at the foot of Whitehead Street is the **Key West Aquarium** (daily 10am–6pm). For a small admission charge, the aquarium offers a vast selection of marine specimens, from both the Gulf waters and the Atlantic Ocean, and a touch tank of starfish, hermit crabs, and horse conches into which you can dip your hand. About a block away, also on Whitehead Street, is the **Audubon House and Gardens** (daily 9.30am–5pm), an antique-filled, three-story home built in the mid-1840s in honor of the American ornithologist James John Audubon. Ironically, given that the Audubon Society conservation group was named in honor of him, Audubon was an enthusiastic hunter of birds and animals. He never actually set foot in this house, which is one of the island's architectural gems.

Hemingway's Menagerie

Farther along Whitehead Street, about six short blocks from the Audubon House and always full of tourists, is **Hemingway House** (daily 9am–5pm), a majestic coral rock mansion with a wrought-iron second-story balcony. It was here that the Nobel Prize-winning author wrote *Death in the Afternoon*, *To Have and Have Not*, and *The Snows of Kilimanjaro*. Hemingway lived here in the 1930s with his wife Pauline, their two sons, a nurse, and a cook. For a small entrance fee, you can join a 30-minute narrated tour, taking in his study, trophies, antiques, and

Above: a six-toed cat at Hemingway's House
Left: it's never dull on Duval Street

the six-toed cats descended from Hemingway's personal menagerie. Sometimes kittens are made available for adoption – there's a five-year waiting list of devoted Hemingway fans. The swimming-pool in the courtyard was supposedly Key West's first.

Down the block, on the other side of the street is the **Lighthouse Museum** (daily 9.30am–5pm). Built in 1847, the 92ft- (28 meter-) high lighthouse and adjacent keeper's home are now a museum filled with nautical charts, antique photographs, and lighthouse paraphernalia. A climb up the 98 lighthouse steps, although exhausting, gives you a panoramic view of the island.

After walking about six more blocks on Whitehead Street toward the dead-end water's edge, you will come across a massive concrete marker, shaped like a buoy with red, black, and yellow bands around it. This is the **Southernmost Point** in the continental US. While the marker itself is not much to look at, countless numbers of tourists pose in front of it for photographs every day of the year.

Cuban Heritage Museum

Parallel to and one block away from Whitehead is **Duval Street**, the main commercial thoroughfare and the liveliest street in the city. A mile-long strip of bars, guesthouses, restaurants, ice-cream parlors, art galleries, and gift shops, Duval is a non-stop circus anytime of the day or night. As you follow Duval, you will be heading back to your starting point. One of the first spots to visit on Duval is the **San Carlos Institute** (Tues–Sun 11am–5pm; small entrance fee), a Cuban heritage museum, theater, and cultural center. Founded in 1871, it focuses on the contribution that Cuban exiles have made to Key West and is housed in a beautifully restored historic building. Check out the hand-painted tiles for which Cuban craftsmen are famous.

Also on this block is the **Strand Theater**, an elaborately designed movie house built by Cuban craftsmen in 1918. Today the Strand, with its ornately decorated facade, serves as home to the **Ripley's Believe It Or Not!** museum (daily 9am–11pm), a so-called 'odditorium' with displays that include shrunken heads, a hurricane wind tunnel, and antique diving gear. Across the street from the Strand is one of Key West's many synthetic attractions – the **Margaritaville Café** (daily 11am–4am). Here, owner Jimmy Buffet, the local pop-folk music hero and sometime Key West resident, has created a shrine to himself and his music. In addition to its trademark frosty margaritas, the café sells Jimmy Buffet souvenirs including recordings, books and even Margaritaville underwear. If you happen to be a diehard Buffet fan, you might decide to stop here for one of the renowned 'Cheeseburger in Paradise' lunches. Otherwise save your hunger pangs for lunch at Sloppy Joe's later *(see Page 70)*.

One block away from the Margaritaville Café is the stately **St Paul's Episcopal Church**. Damaged by three hurricanes, St Paul's was rebuilt with sturdy masonry

Right: the end of the road

work in 1919. Continuing on to the 300 block of Duval Street is the **Wreckers Museum** (Mon–Sat 10am–4pm, Sun noon–4pm), which occupies the oldest house in Key West. Antiques from the 18th century and historic photographs record the days when Key West's notorious pirates raided the ships that were supposedly 'wrecked' offshore and brought their booty to town.

Near the end of Duval are two of the most-talked about spots in Key West. **Sloppy Joe's** (daily 9am–4am) at the corner of Duval and Green Streets, claims to have been Hemingway's favorite drinking hole. A boisterous good-time bar with Hemingway memorabilia on the walls and peanut shells on the floor, Sloppy Joe's is a great place for a late lunch of conch chowder. The bar, however, has been at this location only since the late 1930s; before that, the 'real' Sloppy Joe's where Hemingway went was a block away on Greene Street at what is now **Captain Tony's Saloon** (daily 10am–4am).

The Oldest Bar in Town

Captain Tony's was for decades owned by Tony Tarracino, a former gambler, bootlegger, and boat captain, and is the oldest bar in Key West. Built in 1852, the structure once served as the city morgue. Dark, dank, and outlandish, the bar hasn't changed much in 50 years. Tarracino sold the bar in 1988, and a year later he was elected mayor of Key West. Although he was good at cutting through bureaucratic red tape, Tarracino had a vulgar, saloon-owner style that did not sit well with many of the town's more conservative residents and he was not re-elected. Both Captain Tony's and Sloppy Joe's are great venues in which to pass a relaxing Key West afternoon.

Key West's most vital happening is the sunset celebration. At the foot of Duval, on the waterfront, **Mallory Square** is a pier and park that erupts each evening into a free-spirited party. From about half an hour before dusk, thousands of people congregate to watch the sun sink into the Gulf. Of the street performers who entertain the crowds, some of the more creative acts

the florida keys

include a fire-eating sword-swallower, a Houdini-like character who binds himself in chains and then laboriously wiggles free, and a cat-tamer who has trained domestic cats to jump through flaming hoops.

Beyond Duval and Whitehead streets, the island has several neighborhoods well worth seeking out. One such area, which stretches for several blocks in Old Town, is **Bahama Village** on the southwest side of Whitehead Street. In the 18th century numerous workers from the nearby Bahama Islands settled in Key West, and they went on to play a significant role in building the city. The Bahamians' knowledge of tropical architecture and foliage was put to good use in giving Key West a Caribbean atmosphere. Much of the city's substantial Bahamian population still lives in this neighborhood.

Throughout Bahama Village, you'll find wooden houses, painted in bright shades of pink, blue, and green, and small grocery stores that stock Bahamian specialties. One of the most popular meeting places is **Blue Heaven** (Wed–Sun 8am–3pm, 6–10pm) at the junction between Thomas and Petronia streets. Housed in a three-story Greek Revival clapboard structure, this is a very casual Bahamian/Caribbean restaurant serving curried fish and conch. In the past the building has served as a bordello, a boxing ring, and as a cock-fighting arena. One corner of the property contains a rooster graveyard.

On the other side of Old Town, on Duncan Street near the corner of Leon Street, you will find the **Tennessee Williams Home** in the middle of a dense residential neighborhood. This modest, white-frame house with tomato-red shutters is now a private residence and is not open to the public. The Pulitzer Prize-winning playwright, best known for his works *A Streetcar Named Desire*, *The Glass Menagerie*, and *Night of the Iguana* – all of which were adapted for Hollywood movies in the 1950s and '60s – lived and wrote here for 34 years prior to his death in 1983.

Irreverent Epitaphs

About 10 blocks away from the Tennessee Williams Home, the **Key West Cemetery** on Angela Street is worth visiting. Established in 1847, it is now crowded with overground vaults. Shade is provided by the frangipani, sausage, and palm trees. Look out for the inscriptions on the tombs, a number of which are as irreverent as Key West itself. Among the darkly humorous examples are: *I Told You I Was Sick*, *The Buck Stops Here*, and *Here Lies My Heart*. One of the tombs contains the remains of Elena Hoyos Mesa, a beautiful Cuban woman who suffered the unwanted attentions of a deranged admirer named Karl von Cosel.. Von Cosel was so obsessed by her that, after Elena's death in the 1930s, he dug up her corpse, covered the body with wax, dressed it in a wedding gown, and kept it in his home for seven years before the authorities discovered the grisly scene and returned the body to its tomb.

Above Left: in the spirit of Hemingway.
Left: the sunset from Mallory Pier. **Above:** in Bahama Village

A Day at the Beach

If you have time for a second day in Key West, you might opt for some serious relaxation. Although better known for its uniquely hybrid forms of architecture and its offbeat, bohemian character, Key West is an island of

beautiful public beaches, especially on the southern side of the peninsula. They're frequently covered with seaweed and chunks of coral – and the offshore waters don't reach the depths required for serious swimming – but the beaches should satisfy anyone's desire to bake themselves in the sun's heat, and are worth a day of your time after the diverse sights of the city have been explored.

Most of Key West's public beaches are open from sunrise to sunset and charge a fee only for parking. However, the locals like to squeeze in a day at the beach as part of their weekly schedule, so they are often very crowded. Don't forget to pack a large towel and adequate sun-block lotion. Most of the beaches are well served by food and drink vendors, but a lunch packed in town beforehand is bound to be more satisfying.

At the foot of White Street is the **White Street Pier**, a very popular fishing and sunbathing spot. Opposite the pier, to the left along South Roosevelt Boulevard, is **Smathers Beach**, the longest beach on the island. Smathers is usually teeming with beautiful young windsurfers, bathers, and kite-flyers. In the distance, about a mile away from Smathers Beach near the Key West airport, you should be able to see the **East Martello Tower** (daily 9.30am–5pm), an enormous, brick fort that dates back to the Civil War. Today the tower houses a museum of art and history under the aegis of the Key West Art and Historical Society. On your return journey from the beach you might well decide to stop at the museum, which features exhibitions on pirating, sponging, and turtling, and displays on local artists and writers.

On the right side of the White Street Pier you will find **Higgs Beach**, the second-largest beach on the island.

Complete with a number of picnic tables and a playground, Higgs Beach is particularly popular among families with small children. A thick grove of Australian pine trees provides respite from the sun. At the end of Vernon and Waddell Streets is a small public beach which welcomes both topless bathers and dogs. Around the **Fort Zachary Taylor State Historic Site**, near the Truman Annex at the western end of the island, is a family beach with picnic tables and barbecue grills.

Above: sporting options
Right and Far Right: beach pleasures

Leisure Activities

SHOPPING

Florida offers an array of affordable goodies to take home. Aside from the tacky tourist traps – of which there are thousands – where rubber alligators, Mickey Mouse ears and orange perfume comprise the bulk of the stock, there are stores that sell designer clothes at factory prices, primitive Caribbean art, and sand-polished shells that smell of the ocean. Surprisingly, Florida is a good place for antiques due to the many transplanted retirees who hauled their life's belongings with them. Estate sales, advertised in local newspapers, are often a collector's delight. In addition, many antique dealers from around the country set up shop in Florida dfuring the winter months. Hours may vary, but most shopping centers are open seven days a week.

Orlando

The **Belz Factory Outlet Mall** (Mon–Sat 10am–9pm, Sun 10am–6pm; 5401 West Oakridge Road at the northern end of International Drive; tel: 407-352 9600), the second most-visited 'attraction' in Orlando after Disney World, is a bargain bonanza. This large, indoor mall is made up of four buildings that house almost 100 stores. Belz is the best place in Florida to shop for designer clothes – Anne Klein, London Fog, Christian Dior and many more – and just about every brand of blue jeans, sneakers and casual wear at discounts of up to 75 percent off retail prices.

Flea World (Fri–Sun 9am–6pm, Highway 17–92 just north of Orlando; tel: 407-321 1792) calls itself America's largest flea market, and with 1,000 dealers spreading their wares over 100 acres (40 ha), it may well be. Good for garage-sale clean outs, discounted merchandise, Florida antiques.

The sweet and juicy citrus fruits grown in the center of the state are known worldwide, so stop at **Orange World** – everything in the Orlando area seems to be a 'world' of some sort or another – (daily 8am–11pm, 5395 West Irlo Bronson Memorial Highway, Kissimmee, Tel: 407-396 1306) for a squeeze-while-you-wait drink. You can't miss the building – it is shaped like a giant orange – and inside is an assortment of freshly picked fruit, citrus candies and orange blossom honey, all available to be shipped directly to the folks back home.

Tampa/St Petersburg

Baseball is the country's most popular sport, and Florida is its favorite spring training camp site, with St Petersburg established as the baseball capital of the state. Along with being able to watch sports heroes practice their swings and pitches, St Petersburg is the place to shop for baseball memorabilia. **Sportsmasters of West Florida** (Mon–Fri 10.30am–6pm, Sat 10am–2pm) and **Frank's Cards and Collectibles** (Mon–Sat 11am–6pm, 974 58th Street N), are both great places to pick up antique baseball cards, autographed bats and balls, and many an offbeat American sports treasure.

Left: alfresco dining
Right: plenty in store

A good spot for antique hunting in Tampa is the **Interbay Antique Row** (MacDill and El Prado Avenues near Bayshore Boulevard). It's a shopper's paradise, with dozens of stores spread throughout the area selling all kinds of antique furniture, old postcards, art, Art Deco jewelry and vintage clothing.

St Augustine

Similar to the Orlando area, St Augustine is known for its large discount malls. A few miles north of downtown located on the west side of I-95 on Highway Florida 16 is the **St Augustine Outlet Mall** (Mon–Sat 10am–9pm, Sun 10am–6pm, tel: 904-825 555). The mall has almost 100 designer shops, including Brooks Brothers, Ann Taylor, Coach, Levi's, Jones New York, and Calvin Klein. So sprawling is this mall that a free trolley car is available to transport shoppers from one end to the other. Nearby on the east side of I-95 is a **Belze Factory Outlet Mall** (tel: 904-826 1311) that is almost identical to the one located in Orlando.

In the heart of the St Augustine historic district, the brick-paved Aviles Street and George Street both have an interesting collection of art galleries, antique shops, and clothing boutiques.

Miami

For upscale shopping, one of Miami's most elegant centers is the **Bal Harbour Shops** (Mon–Sat 10am–9pm, Sun noon–6pm; 9700 Collins Avenue, Bal Harbour, tel: 305-866 0311) at the northern end of Miami Beach. The beautiful and elegant center houses Neiman Marcus, Gucci, Fendi, and Ann Taylor boutiques, and offers fine al fresco dining.

If you're after a bargain, it's worth a trip out of Miami to nearby Opa-Locka, site of one of the largest flea markets in South Florida. At the **Opa-Locka/Hialeah Flea Market** (daily 5am–7pm; free parking Mon–Fri), more than 1,200 wholesale and retail vendors showcase their stuff. There are also more than a dozen restaurants featuring international cuisine and beer. The flea market attracts large crowds year-round. Selling everything from dolls to dishes, it's the place to check out for anyone who is working on a particular hobby or amassing a collection.

Key West

Along with drinking silly rum concoctions with paper umbrellas in them, shopping is one of the most popular pastimes in Key West. While everyone agrees that in recent years the town has become cluttered with far too many T-shirt shops, Key West also has a funky collection of art galleries, shell boutiques and jewelry stores. **Key West Aloe** (daily 9am–8pm, 524 Front Street, tel: 305-294 5592) produces hundreds of perfumes, sunscreens and skin care products from the native aloe plant. The products are all natural and refreshing, and aloe gel is one of the best remedies for sunburn. The company's factory, a few blocks from the shop, is open to the public for tours.

At **Key West Hand Print Fabrics** (daily 10am–6pm, 201 Simonton Street, tel: 305-294 9535) workers make brightly colored, hand-printed cotton and silk fabrics that are sold by the yard and as casual clothing. **Fast Buck Freddie's** (daily 10am–6pm, 500 Duval Street, tel: 305-294 2007), a Key West institution, is a department store that specializes in the bizarre – sequined bikinis, battery-operated alligators that bite, and fish-shaped shoes. The **Haitian Art Company** (daily 10am–6pm, 600 Frances Street, tel: 305-296 8932) features one of the largest collections of paintings, sculptures, steel and papier-mâché art imported from Haiti in the US. The **Gingerbread Square Gallery** (daily 11am–6pm, 901 Duval Street, Tel: 305-296 8900), the oldest gallery in Key West, features nationally prominent Key West artists.

Left: checking the local produce

EATING OUT

In recent years, a new wave of cooking, using local tropical ingredients in all sorts of *nouvelle* styles, has surged through Florida's restaurants. Today's chefs combine coconut, citrus, mangoes, and green bananas with fresh, native seafood such as grouper, snapper, pompano, conch, oysters, lobster, shrimp and crab.

Many immigrants from countries such as Cuba, Jamaica, Peru, Nicaragua, Thailand, and Vietnam have in the past 15 years or so carved out a niche in the restaurant scene and their ethnic specialties are now a part of the Florida dining experience. Moreover, Florida, one of the largest cattle producing states in the country, is a sure bet for a good steak or juicy prime rib dinner.

Old-fashioned Florida dining, the kind that existed before mass tourism became the norm, can still be found at small, mom-and-pop cafés in inland areas, and usually means fried catfish and cornmeal hush puppies, grilled alligator tail, frogs' legs, heart of palm salad, and Seminole Indian fried bread. For big eaters on a budget, Florida is the land of the Early Bird Special, a three-course meal usually offered at a reduced price between 4 and 6pm. Sunday buffet brunches, and all-you-can-eat specials are also popular.

Price categories listed below are based on the average cost of a three-course meal without drinks.

$ = under $15

$$ = $15–25

$$$ = over $25.

Gratuities are not usually included in the bill. The best domestic wines tend to come from California or New York, and range in price from $10 to $50 per bottle.

Orlando

Mel's American Graffiti Drive-in

1000 Universal Studios Plaza
Universal Studios
Orlando
Tel: 407-363 8766

Of the many theme restaurants to be found on the periphery of the Universal Studios complex, Mel's American Graffiti Drive-in, with its heavy emphasis on '50s decor and food, is one of the better ones. $

Le Coq Au Vin

4800 South Orange Avenue
Orlando
Tel: 407-851 6980

Considered the finest French restaurant in central Florida. Specialties include rainbow trout with champagne, roast duckling, and chicken liver pâté. $$$

Above: traditional Florida specialties at a fast food outlet

Barney's Steak & Seafood
1615 East Colonial Drive
Orlando
Tel: 407-896 6864
Enormous salad bar, prime cuts of beef and seafood creations in a family atmosphere. **$$**

Power House
111 East Lyman Avenue
Winter Park
Tel: 407-645 3616
Inexpensive and healthy food with a 1960s feel and taste, a half-block from trendy Winter Park's Park Avenue. The herb tea and sandwiches are excellent. **$**

Fort Liberty
5260 West Irlo Bronson Memorial Boulevard
Kissimmee
Tel: 407-351 5151 (ask for restaurant)
A Wild West, cowboys and Indians dinner show restaurant. The food is all-American (typical fare is fried chicken and corn-on-the-cob), as is the shoot-'em-dead floor show. Make reservations. **$$$**

Tampa/St Petersburg
Skippers Smoke House
910 Skipper Road
Tampa
Tel: 813-971 0666
Florida and Caribbean specialties – curried chicken, smoked oysters, gatortail and shark in a rustic setting surrounded by oaks. **$$**

Bern's Steak House
1208 South Howard Avenue
Tampa
Tel: 813-251 2421
Bern's Steak House offers prime cuts of beef, organic vegetables, and more than 7,000 bottles of wine to choose from. Reservations are highly recommended. **$$$**

Leverock's Seafood House
10 Corey Avenue
St Pete Beach
Tel: 727-367 4588
Inexpensive and casual seafood dining. A local favorite. **$**

Outback Steakhouse
4088 Park Street North
St Petersburg
Tel: 727-384 4329
The Outback Steakhouse serves grilled shrimp and massive steaks with a Down Under Australian attitude. **$$**

Columbia Restaurant
2117 East 7th Avenue
Ybor City
Tel: 813-248 4961
After almost a century in business – it was established in 1905 – the Columbia Restaurant continues to specialize in fine Spanish cuisine, with an ambience to match: don't miss the flamenco dance show in the background. **$$**

Crawdaddy's
2500 Rocky Point Drive
Tampa
Tel: 813-281 0407
A popular locals' hangout that serves up gatortail and French fries, Crawdaddy's is known for its funky atmosphere. **$**

St Augustine
Raintree
102 San Marco Avenue
Tel: 904-824 7211
Housed in a grand, historic Victorian mansion, this award-winning eatery with a charming atmosphere specializes in terrific seafood, and a classic beef Wellington. Raintree also features a coffee and dessert bar with made-to-order crepes. **$$$**

Salt Water Cowboy's
299 Dondanville Road
St Augustine Beach
Tel: 904-471 2332
Overlooking a saltwater marsh, Salt Water Cowboy's is lively and inexpensive local restaurant that has the atmosphere of an old-fashioned rustic fishing camp, complete with both indoor and outdoor dining. Specialties on the menu include fried catfish, raw oysters and clams, grilled shrimp, and barbecued beef ribs. **$**

Miami

Puerto Sagua
700 Collins Avenue
Miami Beach
Tel: 305-673 1115
Characterful, with hearty Cuban food. $

Snapper's Restaurant
Bayside Marketplace
Miami
Tel: 305-379 0605
Seafood, steaks, and pasta with a waterfront view. Casual dining. $$

Southfork Cafe
3301 Rickenbacker Causeway
Key Biscayne
Tel: 305-365 9391
Tex-Mex specialties at a downtown marina with live Caribbean music. $$

Los Ranchos
401 Biscayne Boulevard
Miami
Tel: 305-375 8188
Terrific Nicaraguan specials in downtown's Bayside Marketplace. $$

Sundays On The Bay
5420 Crandon Boulevard
Key Biscayne
Tel: 305-361 6777
Miami's best bayfront view and a grand, Sunday buffet brunch. $$

Versailles Restaurant
3555 SW 8th Street
Miami
Tel: 305-444 0240
Little Havana gem, typical Cuban cuisine. Try the roast pork with fried bananas. $

Ft Lauderdale

Burt & Jacks
Berth 23, Port Everglades
Tel: 954-522 5225
Elegant hideaway with breathtaking views, Burt & Jacks features 'man-size' steaks, grilled seafood, and a fine wine list. $$

East City Grill
505 North Ft Lauderdale Beach Boulevard
Tel: 954-565 5569
Multicultural nouvelle cuisine. $$$

Key West

Louie's Backyard
700 Waddell Avenue
Tel: 305-294 1061
American, Caribbean cuisine in romantic, seaside setting. Old Key West ambience. $$$

A & B Lobster House
700 Front Street
Tel: 305-294 5880
Casual seafood, beautiful harbor view. $$

Sunset Pier
Zero Duval Street
Tel: 305-296 7701
A relaxed, T-shirts and sandals kind of place that specializes in conch fritters, smoked fish, and frosty bottled beers. $

Café des Artistes
1007 Simonton Street
Tel: 305-294 7100
An intimate and elegant setting noted for its classic French/tropical specialties such as lobster in cognac sauce and shrimp in mango butter. Reservations required. $$$

Above: immigrants have introduced a new wave of cooking styles

NIGHTLIFE

Although the plentiful sunlight is what draws most travelers to Florida, the state does not lack big-city, bright-light entertainment. Nightlife activities are abundant and the options stretch across a broad range: romantic dinner cruises, Broadway plays, reggae bars, comedy clubs, classical ballet, flamenco shows, beach parties, gay discos, symphony orchestras, and open-air saloons.

In fall and winter months, nationally prominent entertainers make their way south and big-name acts can be found in most of Florida's large cities. Calypso kings and salsa queens from the Caribbean often visit the state at this time of year, which is also the season to catch performances by local orchestras, theaters and dance troupes.

Throughout the year, you will find plenty of nightclubs at which you can dance till the early hours. A number of bars offer karaoke nights and girls' wet T-shirt contests.

Attire for most evening events – classical music concerts, dance performances and theatrical productions notwithstanding – is usually very casual. The minimum drinking age is 21 and identification is required.

Orlando
Carr Performing Arts Center
401 Livingston Street
Orlando
Tel: 407-849 2070
An auditorium that hosts regional and national music, theater and dance troupes.

Orlando Arena
600 West Amelia Street
Tel: 407-849 2070
The Orlando Arena is one of the most important entertainment venues for diverse evening events and concerts in Orlando and the surrounding area.

Rivership Romance
433 North Palmetto
Sanford
Tel: 407-321 5091
Situated about 15 miles (24km) north of Orlando near I-4, the Rivership Romance is located aboard a Southern-style paddlewheel boat that features dinner and dancing cruises along the St John's River. Reservations are required.

Hard Rock Café Orlando
5401 South Kirkman Road
Orlando
Tel: 407-351-ROCK
The international Hard Rock Café chain has brought its rock-and-roll formula to Florida and the young people love it.

Pleasure Island
Disney Village
Lake Buena Vista
Tel: 407-934 7781
This six-acre (2½-ha) complex of nightlife entertainment incorporates seven nightclubs, plus a number of movie theaters, restaurants, a comedy club, and, perhaps best of all, a rock-and-roll beach club.

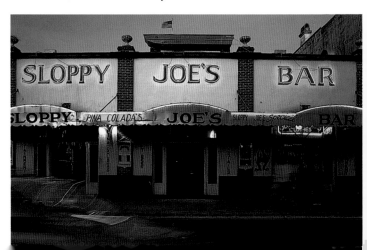

Phineas Phogg's Balloon Works
129 West Church Street
Orlando
Tel: 407-422 2434
A popular, pulsating disco that attracts tourists as well as locals.

Hoop-Dee-Doo Revue
Disney Village
Lake Buena Vista
Tel: 407-934 7639
A corny, but lively, family show full of singing, dancing and clowning around.

Tampa/St Petersburg
Starlite Princess
3400 Pasadena Avenue South
St Petersburg
Tel: 727-367 7804
Dinner and dancing cruises along the Intracoastal Waterway aboard a triple-deck ship.

Tampa Theater
711 Franklin Street
Tampa
Tel: 813-274 8981
A restored 1926 movie palace that offers concerts, foreign films and special events.

Tampa Bay Performing Arts Center
1010 North MacInnes Place
Tampa
Tel: 813-222 1000
One of the largest such centers in Florida, the Tampa Bay Performing Arts Center features three theaters that host a variety of both classical and popular entertainment.

Joyland Country Night Club
11225 US19
St Petersburg
Tel: 727-573 1919
As its name suggests, the Joyland is a Country & Western music and dance club. Cowboy boots suggested.

Coliseum Ballroom
534 4th Avenue North
St Petersburg
Tel: 727-892 5202
The Coliseum is a late-night popular music dance club that occasionally features old-fashioned ballroom dancing.

Cha Cha Coconuts
City Pier
St Petersburg
Tel: 727-822 6655
Cha Cha Coconuts is known for its live jazz concerts, with the water as a spectacular backdrop.

Florida West Coast Symphony
Tel: 727-953 4252
A regional orchestra that performs guest turns at several venues in the area.

Ruth Eckerd Hall
1111 McCullen Booth Road Clearwater
Tel: 727-791 7400
Located just to the north of St Petersburg, the Ruth Eckerd Hall hosts all types of musical events, from rock and roll to symphony concerts, all year round.

Miami
Miami City Ballet
Tel: 305-532 4800
Miami City Ballet is a Latin-flavored classical ballet company with hints of jazz and modern dance. Various Miami locations.

New World Symphony
Tel: 305-673 3330
A first-rate repertoire of classical music played at various theaters and occasionally in the city's moonlit, waterfront parks.

Left: Ernest Hemingway's Key West hangout, or probably not
Above: close encounters of the dance-floor kind

Jackie Gleason Theater of the Performing Arts
1700 Washington Avenue
Miami Beach
Tel: 305-673 7300
The Jackie Gleason Theater is an ultra-modern venue that stages Broadway plays from Sept through May.

Colony Theater
1040 Lincoln Road
Miami Beach
Tel: 305-674 1026
Located in the Art Deco district, the Colony Theater was a movie house until it was transformed into a cozy theater. Today it stages offbeat musical and theatrical performances.

Tobacco Road
626 South Miami Avenue
Miami
Tel: 305-374 1198
Appropriately taking its name from a well-known song, this is a wonderful old, smoke-filled saloon that is particularly good for late-night live jazz and blues bands.

Bacchanallia
1450 Collins Avenue
Miami Beach
Tel: 305-531 4499
A place-to-be-seen gay dance club for those who like to play at dressing up.

Cafe Nostalgia
2212 SW 8 Street
Little Havana
Tel: 305-541 2631
A dark and romantic cafe dedicated to old Cuba with sizzling live salsa, Afro-Cuban jazz, and fancy footwork on the dance floor.

Les Violins
1751 Biscayne Boulevard
Miami
Tel: 305-371 8668
A flashback to Havana 1955, this late-night dinner club puts on a sequin and feathers floor show with lots of Latin flamboyance.

Key West
Tennessee Williams Fine Arts Center
5901 Junior College Road
Tel: 305-296 1520
A 490-seat theater that presents plays, dance, classical and jazz concerts year-round.

Waterfront Playhouse
Mallory Square
Tel: 305-294 5015
This 19th-century salvage warehouse now hosts comedy and dramatic acts Nov–May.

Celebrities
430 Duval Street
Tel: 305-296 4600
Housed in La Concha Holiday Inn, this piano bar is popular with locals and is easy to find.

Havana Docks Lounge
1 Duval Street
Tel: 305-296 4600
A second-floor waterfront disco where locals and tourists come to dance the night away and watch the fish under the harbor lights.

The Green Parrot
400 Southard Street
Tel: 305-294 6133
A well-known hangout with pool tables and darts boards, the Green Parrot is on the raunchy side but full of local color.

The Chart Room
1 Duval Street
The Pier House Hotel
Tel: 305-296 4600
Dark and atmospheric and a tad expensive, the Chart Room is a popular gathering place for sophisticated late-night locals.

Sloppy Joe's Bar
Corner of Duval and Green Streets
Tel: 305-294 5717
One of the best-known night spots in Key West, Sloppy Joe's claims – somewhat dubiously – to have been Hemingway's hangout. This boisterous, good-time bar is replete with Hemingway memorabilia.

CALENDAR OF EVENTS

January – February

The **Festival of the Epiphany** on Jan 6 is the Greek Orthodox celebration of Christ's baptism. Florida's largest Greek community, in Tarpon Springs, north of Tampa, marks the event with a festival (tel: 727-937 3540).

South Miami Beach's **Art Deco Weekend** in mid-Jan attracts Deco-lovers from around the country for a weekend of sidewalk art shows, 1920s big-band music and dancing under the stars (tel: 305-672 2014).

In Feb, Tampa's **Gasparilla Festival** is a month-long party of parades and plays about José Gaspar, a pirate who terrorized sailors in Tampa Bay (tel: 813-223 1111).

Mid-Feb brings two events to Miami. The **Miami Film Festival**, a 10-day celebration of foreign, American and Florida films at venues throughout the city, attracts actors, directors and buffs (tel: 305-539 3000). The **Coconut Grove Arts Festival**, the state's largest, spills onto the streets with a backdrop of live music (tel: 305-447 0401).

March – May

Carnaval Miami (early Mar), the nation's largest Hispanic festival, draws salsa-lovers from around the Americas. Over a million people turn out for a week-long music, dance and food event ending in a 23-block street party in Little Havana (tel: 305-644 8888).

The **Conch Republic Celebrations** (late Apr, early May) honors the founding fathers of Key West (tel: 305-294 4440).

June – July

The **Miami/Bahamas Goombay Festival**, (first weekend in June), claims to be the US's largest black-heritage street fair. Coconut Grove's Bahamian community hosts an island-style bash with Caribbean music, spicy seafood, and potent rum. Originally linked to the freeing of the Bahamas' slaves, the Goombay celebrations are known for their costumed 'Junkanoo' characters and raucous good times (tel: 305-372 9966).

Mid-July's **Hemingway Days Festival** is Key West's tribute to its favorite adopted son. The week-long party includes a literary conference, short-story competitions, a Papa Hemingway lookalike contest, and plenty of machismo madness (tel: 305-294 4440).

October – December

Fantasy Fest in late Oct is Key West at its zaniest. The week-long bacchanalian bash starts with mask-making workshops and costume competitions, and ends with a dusk parade on Halloween night. There's even a pet masquerade contest (tel: 305-294 4440).

Light Up Orlando, on the second Sat in Nov, is when downtown Orlando demonstrates to its theme-park neighbors that it too has something to boast about. The city hosts an evening party with country music, fireworks, ethnic foods and roaming clowns (tel: 407-648 4010).

During the Christmas holiday season, waterways throughout Florida are aglow with twinkling lights as evening boat parades with Santas waving from the decks bring on the Yuletide spirit.

New Year's Eve celebrations are everywhere. One of the grandest is Miami's **King Orange Jamboree Parade** (tel: 305-539 3063). The nationally televised spectacle of glitter and pomp ushers in the New Year with a celebrity lineup that snakes its way through downtown Miami.

Above: the Miami/Bahamas Goombay Festival

Practical
Information

GETTING THERE

More than 40 million people, Americans and foreigners, travel to Florida every year. Lots of Americans, especially those from the colder Midwestern states, consider a winter vacation in Florida to be a birthright, and a trip to the Sunshine State is regarded as a pleasure-seeking form of pilgrimage. In recent years holidaymakers from Europe, South America, and Japan have also added Florida to their list of desired destinations.

By Air

Most air travelers arrive at one of the state's four largest international airports:
- Orlando Airport (tel: 407-825 2000)
- Tampa Airport (tel: 813-870 8700)
- Fort Lauderdale/Hollywood Airport (tel: 954-359 1200)
- Miami Airport (tel: 305-876 7515).

Key West International Airport (tel: 305-296 5439) is a small, regional airport that receives flights from Miami and elsewhere in the state. For departing international flights at all airports, check-in time is 90 minutes prior to take-off. For domestic flights it's one hour.

By Rail

The AMTRAK (tel: 1-800-USA-RAIL) train company brings travelers from around the country. Its major stops in Florida include Tallahassee, Jacksonville, Orlando, Tampa, St Petersburg and Miami. Although not much cheaper than flying, AMTRAK offers views of the countryside on comfortable trains with sleeping bunks and dining-cars.

By Road

Although Florida's state highway system makes for rather boring drives, it's efficient, safe and well-maintained. Gas stations and rest stops are conveniently located, and the road signs are relatively easy to follow. The main north/south routes are I-75, I-95, and the Florida Turnpike, which is a toll road, so be sure to have small change. Coming from the west, the main route is I-10. Good road maps can be obtained free by writing to the Florida Department of Commerce, Collins Building, Tallahassee, FL 32303.

The two main bus companies that service Florida from other parts of the country are Greyhound and Trailways. Both companies have bus stops in all major cities and also in several smaller centers. Although the service is perfectly adequate, many of the bus stops are located in neighborhoods where crime is a problem and caution is advised. Regional phone numbers are listed in local telephone directories.

TRAVEL ESSENTIALS

Visas and Customs

Visa and passport requirements vary according to the country of origin and should be obtained through the relevant consulate. Foreigners visiting Florida might be required to declare all items brought into the state to US Customs at the time of arrival. There is no limit on the amount of money or traveler's checks a visitor can bring into or take out of the US, but any amount over US $5,000 must be reported to US Customs. The duty-free allowance for bringing goods into or out of the United States is 1 liter of liquor and 1 carton of cigarettes.

Left: the Art Deco District
Right: the Orange Blossom Special

Average Temperatures

Months	North	Central	South
Dec–Feb	44–68°F	50–72°F	60–76°F
March–May	62–76°F	66–80°F	68–82°F
June–Aug	71–90°F	73–90°F	75–88°F
Sept–Nov	52–72°F	60–76°F	69–84°F

Time Zones

All of Florida operates on Eastern Standard Time except for a small northwest section of the state that runs on Central Standard Time – an hour earlier. During Daylight Savings Time – from the last Sunday in April through the last Sunday in October – clocks are set 1 hour ahead.

When to Visit

Winter is without doubt the optimum time of year for a visit to Florida. In the winter, Americans and Europeans alike flee the cold in droves for vacations in the Sunshine State. Hotel rates are highest in winter; reservations are essential. Summer months, although very hot, are also popular, especially with American families and South Americans. The 'off season' – spring and fall months – is least crowded and least expensive.

Weather

From the northernmost border to Key West in the south, Florida has a moderate range of temperatures. Clear, sunny skies prevail year-round except for the summer months when afternoon thunderstorms and lightning strikes are common. More people are killed by lightning in Florida than in any other state. If you see lightning, the best advice is to head indoors; if you're driving, stay in your car. The humidity rate is generally high, and in summer months it soars – be prepared for a climate that resembles a mild steam bath.

Hurricanes, as south Florida frequently discovers to its cost, do happen. Florida's hurricane season – the times when a storm is most likely to strike – is June–Oct. Coastal areas are at most risk but inland areas are also vulnerable. The National Weather Service, headquartered in Miami, carefully tracks all possible threats and alerts local communities of any impending danger. Evacuation routes and shelters are available if the threat becomes a reality.

What to Wear

When it comes to clothing, casual is the preferred style in Florida. A few upmarket restaurants require a jacket and tie for men during dinner, but most establishments encourage guests to dress as they please. Shorts, T-shirts and sneakers are acceptable for both men and women, but bathing suits should not be worn beyond the confines of the beach or swimming pool.

In general, lightweight cotton clothing is the most practical form of attire. You should bring a jacket or sweater, even in summer, because air-conditioned restaurants can be as cold as Canada.

Electricity

Standard electrical sockets use a 110-VOLT current; 220-VOLT razor sockets are available at most hotels. Electrical adapters can be purchased at many drugstores, or sometimes borrowed from a hotel concierge.

GETTING ACQUAINTED

Geography and Culture

Florida occupies the southeastern peninsula of the US, with Tallahassee as its capital. Its land area of 58,000 sq miles exceeds that of England. The state measures 450 miles (720km) long by 150 miles (240km) wide, and it has more than 7,000 lakes, 34 rivers,

Above: fun and games on one of Florida's numerous beaches

and 1,000 miles (1,600km) of beaches. Along the east coast lies the Atlantic Ocean, and to the west, the Gulf of Mexico. Its southernmost point is just 1,700 miles (2,720km) north of the equator.

Most of the state is flat, flat, flat. But in parts of central and northern Florida there are hills, albeit not very big ones. Oak, pine and cypress trees cover much of the rural land; south of the Palm Beach County line palm trees and tropical plants are abundant.

Florida's nickname, the 'Sunshine State', was officially designated by the state's legislature in 1970. The orange blossom is the state flower, the mockingbird the state bird. The state song is *Old Folks at Home*, commonly known as *Suwannee River*.

With a fast-growing population that currently stands at just over 13 million, Florida no longer fits the *Old Folks At Home* image. The state's reputation as a retirement haven is fading, as a result of a recent influx of youthful immigrants and families from around the country, which has turned Florida into a booming sun-belt state.

Its ethnic blend incorporates Native Americans, Hispanics, Jews, West Indians, African-Americans, Yankees (Northerners), and Crackers (old-time Floridians whose ancestors sided with the South during the Civil War). Although it is predominantly a Christian state, denominations of all the world's major religions can be found, along with quite a few New Age sects.

MONEY MATTERS

Cash/Traveler's Checks/Credit Cards

All of Florida's international airports have exchange bureaus that will convert foreign currency. Banks will also exchange currencies. Banking hours are usually Mon–Fri 9am–3pm, but some are open on Sat mornings too. Traveler's checks are accepted at most mainstream establishments, as are major credit cards.

Automatic teller machines (ATMs) that dispense cash 24 hours a day are located in most airports, shopping centers and hotels. Systems available are Cirrus, Plus, Master-Card, Visa, Carte Blanche, Diners Club and American Express.

American Express also features an Express Cash service which allows card-holders to withdraw up to US $2,500 from their personal checking accounts.

The toll-free telephone numbers for lost or stolen cards or traveler's checks are:

Visa 800-336 8472
Mastercard 800-800 4000
American Express 800-441 0519.

Phone numbers for others are listed in local directories.

Taxes

Florida's state sales tax stands at six percent, but several counties within the state add on their own tax, bringing the overall sales tax in some areas to seven percent. There's also a 'bed tax' the rate of which varies from county to county. The bed tax will add another few percent to a hotel room rate.

Tipping

Gratuities are rarely included on restaurant bills; if they are, a notation will draw your attention to the fact. In the majority of cases, the standard tipping rate is somewhere between 15 percent and 20 percent, depending on your discretion and the quality of the service you receive.

Tips for luggage handlers at airports and hotels are usually $1 per bag.

GETTING AROUND

Car

Unfortunately, it is difficult to get around in Florida without a car. Many of the larger hotels offer shuttle services to transport their guests to nearby attractions, but in order to explore on your own you must have transportation. If you're not driving into the state with your own car, it's a good idea to rent one. Valid driver's licenses from other countries are accepted.

Rental car rates in Florida are relatively low and vary between companies. Rates are available per day, week or month and, depending on the season, the price for a small car can range from $75 to $150 per week. Most rental companies don't charge a mileage fee on top of this. Available vehicles include: economical compacts, luxury sedans, vans, motorcycles, motor-homes, campers, and convertibles. A few reliable companies are:

Avis	Tel: (1-800) 331 1212
Budget	Tel: (1-800) 527 0700
Dollar	Tel: (1-800) 307 7309
Hertz	Tel: (1-800) 654 3131
National	Tel: (1-800) 328 4567
Thrifty	Tel: (1-800) 367 2277

Driving Regulations

Speed limits on the highways are 55mph (88kph) or 65mph (104kph) depending on the municipality and road conditions. On the smaller roads the speed limit is between 20mph (32kph) and 40mph (64kph). Road signs indicate the local limits, which are strictly enforced by the local police. Florida law allows drivers to make a right turn at a red light after the vehicle has been brought to a complete stop. Other relevant state laws of which you should be aware if driving include the following provisions: all traffic – on both sides of the street unless it is a divided highway – must stop while a school bus is loading or unloading children; passing is allowed in the left lane only; motorcyclists must wear helmets; and drivers and front-seat passengers must wear seat-belts.

Public Transportation

Public buses are available in most cities; hotel employees should be able to provide you with relevant schedules and also information about routes. Although inexpensive, buses can be time-consuming and somewhat impractical. Tampa and Miami both have public, Metromover train systems that are convenient for sightseeing.

Taxis are available in most cities, but they aren't easy to hail from a street corner. In most cases a phone call in advance is needed for a pick-up. Rates average about $1.25 per mile no matter how many passengers share the car. An additional $1 charge is usually added to airport fares.

HOURS & HOLIDAYS

Business Hours

Most shops and offices are open Mon–Fri 9am–5pm with no closing hours for lunch. Most large shopping centers are open Mon–Sat 10am–9.30pm and Sun 10am–6pm.

Public Holidays

Banks and the majority of businesses are closed during the following public holidays:
Jan 1: New Year's Day
Jan 15: Martin Luther King Day
3rd Monday in Feb: Presidents Day
Last Mon in May: Memorial Day
July 4: Independence Day
1st Mon in Sept: Labor Day
2nd Mon in Oct: Columbus Day
Nov 11: Veterans Day
4th Thur in Nov: Thanksgiving
Dec 25: Christmas Day

Miami Transport

Okeechobee · Hialeah · Tri-Rail · Northside · Earlington Heights · Dr. MLK, Jr · Brownsville · Allapattah · Santa Clara · Civic Center · Culmer · Overtown / Arena · Government Center · Brickell · Vizcaya · Coconut Grove · Douglas Road · University · South Miami · Dadeland North · Dadeland South

School Board · Omni · Bicentennial Park · 11th St · Park West · Arena / State Plaza · College North · Freedom Tower · College / Bayside · Miami Ave · 1st St · Bayfront Park · 3rd St · Knight Centre · Riverwalk · 5th St · 8th St · 10th St Promenade · Brickell · Financial District

Metromover & station
Metrorail & station

Not to Scale

ACCOMMODATIONS

Accommodation in Florida ranges from modern, self-contained resorts to historic inns, youth hostels, and mom-and-pop motels. For general information on where to go contact the Florida Hotel/Motel Association, 200 West College Avenue, Tallahassee, FL 32301; Tel: 850-224 2888. Rates in the following list are for the lowest prices available per night for two people in the winter season:

> $ = under $75
> $$ = $75–150
> $$$ = $150–225
> $$$$ = over $225.

Rates on a weekly basis, and during the slow season, are less expensive.

Orlando
Wyndham Palace Resort
1900 Buena Vista Drive
Lake Buena Vista
FL 32380
Tel: 407-827 2727
One of Disney World's 'official' hotels, Wyndham Palace is a sprawling property with fine features that include more than 1,000 rooms, three swimming pools, three tennis courts, a health club and a number of excellent restaurants. All in all, this is a modern and well-managed hotel. **$$**

Knights's Inn Orlando Maingate West
7475 West Irlo Bronson Highway
Kissimmee
FL 32746
Tel: 407-396 4200
A comfortable budget motel with a pool and non-smoker rooms. **$**

Courtyard at Lake Lucerne
211 North Lucerne Circle East
Orlando
FL 32801
Tel: 407-648 5188
One of the finest inns in the state featuring Victorian antiques, hearty breakfasts, and down-home hospitality. **$$**

The Peabody
9801 International Drive
Orlando
FL 32819
Tel: 407-352 4000
The Peabody is a high-rise, first-class hotel which is particularly recommended for families with children. The hotel's theme is ducks, and every morning a parade of mallards struts through the lobby. **$$$**

Harley Hotel
151 East Washington Street
Orlando
FL 32801
Tel: 407-841 3220
Benefiting from a superb location in downtown Orlando, the Harley is within easy walking distance of all the major downtown attractions, restaurants, and museums. Although it is a bustling place, it is also very comfortable. **$$**

Hostel International Kissimmee Florida
4840 East Irlo Bronson Highway
Kissimmee
FL 32746
Tel: 407-843 8888
Situated within reach of all the Disney action, this budget hostel has 120 dormitory beds plus a few private rooms, and a full common room/kitchen. Guests must be 18 years or older. **$**

Above: one way to travel

Country Hearth Inn
9861 International Drive
Orlando
FL 32819
Tel: 407-352 0008
A warm and friendly mansion/inn with a peaceful atmosphere, private balconies, and a full breakfast each morning. **$$**

Tampa/St Petersburg
Hyatt Regency Downtown
211 North Tampa Street
Tampa
FL 33602
Tel: 813-225 1234
A sophisticated downtown hotel located in the business district, the Hyatt Regency is within easy walking distance of the local shopping centers and museums. **$$**

Bayboro House
1719 Beach Drive SE
St Petersburg
FL 33701
Tel: 727-823 4955
Bayboro House is a traditional, old, gable-roofed inn with rocking chairs on the front porch. Located across the street from Tampa Bay. Quiet, cozy and warm. **$**

The Heritage
234 3rd Avenue North
St Petersburg
FL 33701
Tel: 727-822 4814
A calming bed-and-breakfast inn dedicated to historic preservation in the heart of downtown, the Heritage has a small swimming pool and a popular restaurant. **$$**

Holiday Inn Busch Gardens
2701 East Fowler Avenue
Tampa
FL 33612
Tel: 813-971 4710
A family-oriented motel complete with a swimming pool, exercise room and a restaurant, the Holiday Inn is just a mile from Busch Gardens. **$$**

Hilton Garden Inn
1700 East 9th Avenue
Tampa
FL 33605
Tel: 813-769 9267
Situated right in the heart of Ybor City, this relaxing hotel has full amenity rooms, a fireplace, heated pool, exercise room, whirlpool, and full-service restaurant. **$$**

Gram's Place
3109 North Ola Avenue
Tampa
FL 33603
Tel: 813-221 0596
A small bed & breakfast/artists' retreat house with a music-filled bar. Gram's Place caters to a gay clientele in particular but makes all guests feel welcome. **$**

Travellodge
6300 Gulf Boulevard
St Petersburg beach
FL 33706
Tel: 727-367 2711
Located right on the beach, this sprawling property with a pool caters to families with children and offers rooms and full suites with kitchens. **$$**

St Augustine
Montery Inn
16 Avenida Menendez
St Augustine
FL 32084
Tel: 904-824 4482
A modest but comfortable family-run motel overlooking Matanzas Bay. Good proximity to the historic district and shopping. **$**

Casa Monica Hotel
95 Cordova Street
St Augustine
FL 32084
Tel: 904-827 1888
Dating back to the 19th century, this grand hotel has luxurious rooms and an antique Spanish decor. It also has concierge service, a cocktail lounge, gym, and pool. **$$$**

Right: the pool, the sun, and the architecture are all pure Florida

Carriage Way Bed & Breakfast
70 Cuna Street
St Augustine
FL 32084
Tel: 904-829 2467
Housed in a Victorian home, this quaint B&B is furnished with four-poster beds, clawfoot bathtubs, and an original working fireplace. Full breakfasts each morning. **$$**

Westcott House on the Bay
146 Avenida Menendez
St Augustine
FL 32084
Tel: 904-824 4301
A wood-frame house with a second-floor veranda, fireplaces, brass beds, and a lush courtyard. Near the historic Old Town. **$$**

Miami
Cordozo
1300 Ocean Drive
Miami Beach
FL 33139
Tel: 305-535 6500
Oceanfront, Art Deco hotel in the Art Deco District. Nice rooms, good service. **$$**

Fontainebleau Hilton
4441 Collins Avenue
Miami Beach
FL 33140
Tel: 305-538 2000
Grand 1950s hotel with more than 1,000 rooms, ocean views, health spa, and water-fall swimming-pool. **$$$**

Hyatt Regency Miami
400 SE 2nd Avenue
Miami
FL 33131
Tel: 305-358 1234
A modern, business-district hotel, the Hyatt Regency is within walking distance of down-town shopping. **$$**

Mayfair House
3000 Florida Avenue
Miami
FL 33133
Tel: 305-441 0000
Located in the center of Coconut Grove, the Mayfair is an architectural gem. Luxurious rooms and first-class restaurants. **$$$$**

Miami River Inn
118 SW South River Drive
Miami
FL 33130
Tel: 305-325 0045
A charming hotel with old-time Florida style beside the Miami river in Little Havana. **$$**

The Tides
1220 Ocean Drive
Miami Beach
FL 33139
Tel: 305-604 5000
One of the trendiest hotels on the beach, the 12-story Tides is an Art Deco masterpiece featuring chic rooms, broad ocean views, a freshwater pool, sophisticated service, and a wonderful bar. **$$**

enormous marina, the Hyatt Regency Pier 66 is a luxury resort with a swimming pool, sauna, tennis, health salon, boat rentals, concierge service, and a revolving rooftop restaurant with glorious views. $$$

Caribbean Quarters Bed & Breakfast
3012 Grenada Street
Ft Lauderdale
FL 33304
Tel: 954-523 3226
A friendly and comfortable tropical hide-away with lush gardens, wicker furniture, paddle fans, wrought-iron balconies, and well-stocked kitchens, located just a block away from the beach. $

Banana Bungalow
2360 Collins Avenue
Miami Beach
FL 33139
Tel: 305-538 1951
A great budget getaway with a hostel-like atmosphere, pool, outdoor café, communal kitchen, laundry, and shuffleboard courts. Dormitory-style and private rooms. $

Hampton Inn
2800 SW 28th Terrace
Coconut Grove
FL 33133
Tel: 305-448 2800
A well managed hotel in walking distance from Coconut Grove's art galleries, shopping centers, restaurants, and cafés. $$

Courtyard Villas
4312 El Mar Drive
Lauderdale-By-The-Sea
FL 33308
Tel: 954-776 1164
A romantic and historic hotel with stunning ocean views, rattan furniture, classic Florida decor, a heated swimming pool, and fully equipped kitchens. $$

A Little Inn By The Sea
4546 North Ocean Drive
Ft Lauderdale
FL 33308
Tel: 954-772 2450
A Swiss-run property that is very popular with Europeans, this little inn has a comfortable family atmosphere with pretty rooms and ocean views. $$

Fort Lauderdale
Riverside Hotel
620 E Las Olas Boulevard
Fort Lauderdale
FL 33301
Tel: 954-467 0671
One of the oldest hotels in south Florida, the Riverside is a grand old dame situated in the heart of the downtown area, and surrounded by antique shops, art galleries, cafés, and restaurants. $$

Key Largo
Jules Undersea Lodge
51 Shoreland Road
Key Largo
FL 33037
Tel: 305-451 4789
A somewhat expensive and extremely unusual, if not unique, underwater lodge, the Jules was originally designed to be a research laboratory. It features sleeping quarters for six people and room service three times a day. $$$

Hyatt Regency Pier 66
2301 SE 17th Street Causeway
Ft Lauderdale
FL 33316
Tel: 954-525 6666
Very popular with boaters as a result of its

Above: Pier House in Key West is a luxurious option

Westin Beach Resort
MM 97 Overseas Highway
Key Largo
FL 33037
Tel: 305-852 8669
A plush resort tucked inside lush grounds complete with nature trails, a pool, private balconies and facilities for children. **$$$**

Neptune's Hideaway
MM 104 Overseas Highway
Key Largo
FL 33037
Tel: 305-451 0357
A collection of pretty pink cottages with a private beach and barbecue grills. **$$**

Largo Lodge
MM 105 Overseas Highway
Key Largo
FL 33037
Tel: 305-451 0424
A motor lodge with a private beach, and full kitchen in every room. **$**

Sunset Cove Motel
MM 99.5 Overseas Highway
Key Largo
FL 33037
Tel: 305-451 0705
Dorm-style rooms and private rooms. **$**

Islamorada
Harbor Lights Resort
MM 85 Overseas highway
Islamorada
FL 33036
Tel: 305-664 3611
A simple, pleasant resort with screened porches, pool, and watersports facilities. **$$**

Plantation Key Yacht Harbor
MM 87 Overseas Highway
Islamorada
FL 33036
Tel: 305-852 2381
A bright, white resort with comfortable rooms, tennis courts, pool, private beach, and watersports on the premises. **$$**

Cheeca Lodge
MM 82.5 Overseas Highway
Islamorada
FL 33306
Tel: 305-245 3755
Elegant 200-room resort with golf, tennis, two pools, and a series of lagoons. **$$$**

Key West
Ocean Key House
Zero Duval Street
Key West
FL 33040
Tel: 305-296 7701
A plush, all-suite hotel with water views and Jacuzzis in all rooms. **$$$$**

Pier House
1 Duval Street
Key West
FL 33040
Tel: 305-296 4600
Luxury resort, private beach and beautiful rooms. At the foot of the main street. **$$$$**

The Curry Mansion
511 Caroline Street
Key West
FL 33040
Tel: 305-294 5349
A friendly place, this is a Victorian mansion reborn as a B&B inn. **$$$**

Island City House
422 William Street
Key West
FL 33040
Tel: 305-294 5702
Situated just off the main strip, this tropical garden hotel is a soothing oasis with comfortable rooms. **$$$**

Southernmost Motel
1319 Duval Street
Key West
FL 33040
Tel: 305-294 5539
A quaint motel with a beautiful pool and full-service concierge. **$$**

HEALTH & EMERGENCIES

Medical and Dental Services

Most cities have walk-in medical and dental clinics that will treat you regardless of affiliation or insurance. Payment is expected upon completion of the treatment.

In the case of medical emergencies that require urgent attention, at any time of day or night, you should call the emergency services on 911, and an ambulance will immediately be dispatched. The toll-free number is the same throughout the state, and indeed the country.

The following hospitals offer 24-hour emergency-room care:

Orlando
Orlando Regional Medical Center
9400 Turkey Lake Road, Orlando,
Tel: 407-351 8500

Tampa
University Community Hospital
3100 East Fletcher Avenue, Tampa,
Tel: 813-971 6000

Miami
Jackson Memorial Medical Center
1611 NW 12th Avenue, Miami
Tel: 305-585 1111

Key West
Florida Keys Memorial Hospital
5900 Junior College Road, Key West
Tel: 305-294 5531.

Pharmacies

Most pharmacies are open daily 9am–9pm. The following are open 24 hours:

Eckerd Drugs, 670 Lee Road, Orlando
Tel: 407-644-6908;

Eckerd Drugs, 8925 Terrace Road, Tampa,
Tel: 813-988 5214;

Walgreens, 5731 Bird Road, Miami
Tel: 305-666 0757.

Crime

To reach the police in an emergency, from wherever you happen to be in the state, dial 911. Non-emergency police numbers vary according to the city and can be found in the local telephone directory.

Crime constitutes a perennial nuisance that tourism officials wish would go away, but unfortunately it's here to stay. Although, when compared to urban areas in other parts of the country, the crime rate in Florida is relatively low, it does pose all sorts of potential problem for travelers. Criminals can spot tourists without too much difficulty – cameras, sunburned faces, foreign accents, wallets full of money and Mickey Mouse T-shirts are all clear markings that spell out the visitor's vulnerability.

The best advice is to deposit extra cash and jewelry in hotel safes, never leave luggage unattended, and keep a close eye on purses and shoulder bags.

The most recent trend in tourist-related crime targets the drivers of rental cars. Given that most rental cars are conspicuously marked as such, they too tend to attract the attention of criminals. One useful tip that is well worth observing is: if driving alone, never leave a bag on the passenger seat – street robbers have been known to throw rocks through windows while cars are stopped at traffic lights. For added protection, store all valuables in the trunk, while driving or parked.

Although precautions are advisable, you should not let the fear of crime have a negative effect on your vacation. Florida's cities, including Miami, are not as dangerous as their reputation would have it.

COMMUNICATIONS & NEWS

Post

Post office hours vary, but in general they are open Mon–Fri 9am–5pm, Sat 9am–noon. Tourists can have mail delivered to most main post offices by having it sent to their

name in care of General Delivery. Postage stamps are sold at post offices and also at most hotels, pharmacies, airports and super-markets. Overnight delivery services and package deliveries are available courtesy of the US Post Office, United Parcel Service, and Federal Express.

Telephone

Public telephones are located at hotels, gas stations, restaurants, shopping centers and most public places. The toll is 25¢ or 35¢ at all phones in the state. Long-distance calls are at their least expensive on weekends and after 5pm on weekdays.

The main area codes in Florida are 954, 786, 561, 727, 352, 813, 904, 407, 850 and 305. Numbers with an 800 or 888 area code are toll-free. For calls outside the local area codes dial 1 + the area code + the number. For operator assistance dial 0.

To dial other countries, you should first dial the international access code 011, then the country code:

Australia (61)
France (33)
Germany (49)
Italy (39)
Japan (81)
Mexico (52)
Spain (34)
United Kingdom (44).

If using a US phone credit card, dial the company's access number below, then 01, then the country code.

Sprint: 1010333
AT&T: 1010288.

Media

There are more than 100 newspapers across the state. The award-winning *Miami Herald* is the most comprehensive paper in Florida, and the *Orlando Sentinel*, *St Petersburg Times*, and *Tampa Tribune* are also good news sources.

Out-of-state and foreign newspapers can be bought at most newsstands and hotel gift shops. All of the major Florida cities have television stations affiliated with the big national networks, and many hotels offer complimentary cable television with a wide choice of channels.

SPORTS

Fishing

Florida's coastline is an angler's dream. Here you will find more than 600 varieties of fish, including marlin, kingfish, sailfish, dolphin, sea trout and shark. Whether it's deep-sea fishing by boat or surf-casting from the shore, Florida offers excellent salt-water fishing throughout the year. The freshwater

Above: young anglers display their trophies

fishing is also good in the state's numerous waterways – lakes, rivers and streams – and in the Florida Everglades.

Licenses are required for freshwater fishing; for information call the Florida Game and Fresh Water Fish Commission (tel: 850-488 3641). Salt-water fishing does not require a license; for information on fishing areas call the Florida Department of Natural Resources (tel: 850-488 7326). If you forget to pack your rod and reel, you should not have a problem finding a shop that rents fishing equipment by the day.

Tennis

With over 7,700 tennis courts (clay, grass and hard courts), it's little wonder that Florida has become a major sponsor of several international events. The Florida Tennis Association (tel: 954-968 3434) can point you in the direction of the nearest public or private court.

Golf

When it comes to golf, Florida beats all of the country's other states. For information relating to more than 1,000 public and private courses, contact the Florida Sports Foundation (tel: 850-488 8347).

Jai-Alai

Jai-Alai, which enjoys a reputation for being the word's fastest sport, made its way to Florida from the Basque area of Spain and now has a substantial audience. The game, which is similar to handball, is played in courts called frontons, and betting is a part of the fun. For information on any of the eight frontons in Florida, call the Department of Business Regulations (tel: 850-470 5675).

Horse/Dog Racing

For those who appreciate the opportunity to gamble at the racetrack, Florida has thoroughbred horse-racing, harness-racing, and greyhound-racing. For information on tracks, schedules, and betting practices, call the Department of Business Regulations (tel: 850-470 5675).

Other Sports
Scuba Diving
For information throughout the state on this increasingly popular sport, call the Florida Association of Dive Operators (tel: 850-222 6000).
Professional Football
Miami Dolphins (tel: 305-620 2578)
Tampa Bay Buccaneers (tel: 813-879 2827)
Professional Basketball
Miami Heat (tel: 954-835 7000)
Orlando Magic (tel: 407-896 2442)
Professional Baseball
Florida Marlins (tel: 305-626 7400).

USEFUL ADDRESSES

Tourist Offices
The main office for the state's tourism authority is:
Visit Florida
126 West Van Buren Street
Tallahassee, FL 32399
Tel: 850-488 5607.

If you telephone or write to this office in advance of your visit to Florida, staff will forward information packs with all sorts of relevant features. The following are regional tourist offices:

Orlando Official Visitors Center
8723 International Drive, Orlando, FL 32819
Tel: 407-363 5872

Kissimmee/St Cloud Convention and Visitors Bureau
1925 Irlo Bronson Memorial Highway, Kissimmee, FL 34742
Tel: 407-847 5000

Florida's Space Coast Office of Tourism,
2725 St John's Street, Melbourne, FL 32940.
Tel: 321-633 2110

Tampa/Hillsborough Convention & Visitor's Bureau
400 North Tampa Street, Tampa, FL 33602
Tel: 813-223 2752

St Petersburg Chamber of Commerce
PO Box 1371, St Petersburg, FL 33731
Tel: 727-821 4069

St Augustine Chamber of Commerce
1 Riberia Street, St Augustine, FL 32084
Tel: 904-829 6478

Greater Miami Convention & Visitors Bureau
701 Brickell Avenue, Miami, FL 33132
Tel: 305-539 3000

Greater Fort Lauderdale Convention & Visitors Bureau
1850 Eller Drive, Ft Lauderdale, FL 33316
Tel: 954-765 4466

Florida Keys Visitors Center
106000 Overseas Highway, Key Largo, FL 33037
Tel: 305-451 1414

Consulates

All of the following consulate offices are in Miami:

Denmark	305-446 4284
Germany	305-358 0290
United Kingdom	305-374 1522 or
	407-426 7855
Italy	305-374 6322
Canada	305-579 1600

FURTHER READING

Insight Guide: Florida, APA Publications, *2000.* This edition has been expanded and updated with comprehensive descriptions of the sights, background features, and detailed tips on accommodation, travel, eating out and entertainment, plus full-colour maps and stunning photography.

Insight Guide: Miami, APA Publications, *2000.* This edition includes perceptive features, many new images, brand-new maps and up-to-date information on all the sights.

Also includes chapters on the Everglades and Florida Keys.

Insight Pocket Guide: Miami, APA Publications. A companion guide to this volume, featuring the latest information, suggested itineraries and out-of-town excursions.

Insight Pocket Guide: Florida Keys, APA Publications. The 2001 edition features updated information, suggested tours with accompanying maps.

Insight Compact Guide: Florida, APA Publications. This guide is perfect for on-the-spot reference, combining text on places and culture, pictures, and maps in a very user-friendly format.

Insight Compact Guide: Miami, APA Publications. An ideal companion for a visit to Miami, with concise but detailed information, maps and attractive photographs.

Insight Compact Guide: Florida Keys, APA Publications. Covering the south of the state, from Miami to Key West, with nine recommended routes, and updated information on accommodation, restaurants, etc.

Right: an angler's dream

ACKNOWLEDGEMENTS

Photography	
1, 2/3, 5, 8/9, 11, 15, 29, 37, 40, 43, 44, 47T, 51, 52, 53, 55, 56, 70B, 71, 75, 79, 80, 81, 83, 84, 85, 92	**Tony Arruza**
98	**Courtsey of Busch Gardens**
25T, 27	**©Disney**
14B	**Ricardo Ferro**
10, 12B	**Florida Division of Tourism**
31B, 64T	**Photo Courtesy of Florida Keys TDC**
6T, 16, 31T, 48T/B, 54, 59, 62T, 95	**Glyn Genin**
60	**Greater Fort Lauderdale Convention & Visitors Bureau**
73	**Catherine Karnow**
14T, 30, 49, 76, 86	**Bud Lee**
67	**Sugden McCluskey Associates**
68T, 69, 70T	**Monroe County TDC**
12T	**Henry Morrison Fagler Museum**
32	**Orlando Orange County**
28	**Universal Studios Florida**
7T/B, 20, 21, 23, 24, 25B, 26, 33, 34, 35, 36T/B, 39T/B, 41, 42, 58B, 61, 62B, 64B, 77, 91	**Mark Read**
6B, 57, 63, 65, 66, 68B, 72T/B, 89	**Marcus Wilson-Smith**
Cover	**Paul Rees/Tony Stone Images**
Back cover	**NASA**
Cartography	**Berndtson & Berndtson**
	Maria Donnelly

INSIGHT
Pocket Guides

Insight Pocket Guides pioneered a new approach to guidebooks, introducing the concept of the authors as "local hosts" who would provide readers with personal recommendations, just as they would give honest advice to a friend who came to stay. They also included a full-size pull-out map. Now, to cope with the needs of the 21st century, new editions in this growing series are being given a new look to make them more practical to use, and restaurant and hotel listings have been greatly expanded.

Also from Insight Guides...

Insight Guides is the classic series, providing the complete picture with expert and informative text and stunning photography. Each book is an ideal travel planner, a reliable on-the-spot companion – and a superb visual souvenir of a trip. 193 titles.

Insight Maps are designed to complement the guidebooks. They provide full mapping of major destinations, and their laminated finish gives them ease of use and durability. 100 titles.

Insight Compact Guides are handy reference books, modestly priced yet comprehensive. The text, pictures and maps are all cross-referenced, making them ideal books to consult while seeing the sights. 127 titles.

INSIGHT POCKET GUIDE TITLES

INDEX